easy cocktails

easy cocktails

over 200 classic and contemporary recipes

RYLAND
PETERS
& SMALL

LONDON NEW YORK

Designer Paul Tilby
Senior Commissioning Editor Julia Charles
Editor Jo Lethaby
Production Paul Hammond
Art Director Leslie Harrington
Publishing Director Alison Starling

Indexer Hilary Bird

First published in 2011
by Ryland Peters & Small
20–21 Jockey's Fields
London WC1R 4BW
and
Ryland Peters & Small, Inc.
519 Broadway
5th Floor
New York, NY 10012
www.rylandpeters.com

10 9 8 7 6 5 4 3 2 1

UK ISBN: 978 1 84975 163 6
US ISBN: 978 1 84975 164 3

A CIP record for this book is available from the
British Library.

Library of Congress Cataloging-in-Publication Data
has been applied for.

Printed in China.

contents

where it all began

The origin of the cocktail is steeped in colourful myth. The term 'cocktail' first appeared in an American dictionary in 1806 as a 'mixed drink of any spirit, bitters and sugar'.

Where the word cocktail first came from is anyone's guess. Some believe the cocktail was named after an Aztec princess called Xochitl. Others claim it was the innkeeper, Betsy Flanagan, who first coined the phrase. Betsy, they say, would tie chickens' tail feathers to mugs and cry 'Vive le Cock-tail!' to the French soldiers she was serving. Or do its origins lie in the French *coquetel* meaning 'mixed drink'? Whatever the origin of the word, it wasn't until 1920s America that modern cocktail culture really took off.

Although many of the cocktails we now regard as 'classic' were invented before the 20th century, it was really the roaring twenties that saw cocktails come into their own. This happy time coincided with a most unhappy state of affairs in the USA – the social experiment called Prohibition (1920–1933). This era had a number of effects on drinking culture. It forced drinkers underground into illicit bars known as speakeasies. These bars weren't dives though – quite the opposite, they were luxurious and lavishly decorated and much more female friendly, which lent additional glamour to cocktails!

Because liquor was illegal, the inferior bootleg liquor, or moonshine, was drunk, but was often so vile that bartenders would mix it with other juices and syrups to mask its aggressive flavour. The Long Island Iced Tea was created in these times, its seemingly innocuous name designed to fool the authorities. Drinks would also be served in mugs in an effort to distract the hapless police force!

Those bartenders who didn't wish to break the law during Prohibition hotfooted it to Europe or Cuba to ply their trade anew in a different continent, but with as much enthusiasm as ever. This was a particularly creative time for them. Many of the drinks we count as classics today, from the Bloody Mary to the daiquiri, were invented during that period, with the names of the bartenders who created them still hallowed in bars everywhere.

President Franklin D. Roosevelt had other ideas about Prohibition and it was repealed in 1933, shortly after he came to office. An accomplished drinker and handy bartender himself, FDR, along with Winston Churchill, was a great protagonist of, among other cocktails, the martini. Indeed, it was during a summit meeting between Joseph Stalin, Churchill and Roosevelt, in 1943, that Roosevelt first whipped up Dirty Martinis for his companions.

More should be said about the martini in this opening piece. The most iconic of cocktails, this drink has been enjoyed and tinkered with by a greater alumni of politicians, playwrights and playboys than has ever gathered around a bar. And it was these legendary drinkers who made cocktails the stuff of blurred anecdote and folklore, enshrined in times of glamour. Humphrey Bogart's dying words were reported to have been 'I should never have switched from Scotch to martinis' – perhaps not the most encouraging message for non-enthusiasts but a great quote none the less!

Women, never very welcome in bars, were welcomed with open arms to the cocktail lounges of the 1930s. Although there were still laws in some American states prohibiting women from ordering drinks at the bar, this was easily circumvented by implementing table service.

You may imagine that the 1940s bar was a place for reflection and austerity, mirroring the sombre post-war mood. Fortunately, a cocktail can be perfect for times of reflection as well as jubilation. The soldiers returning from the South Pacific to America told tales of the exotic Tiki cocktails made with rum and juices. Such tales prompted a cocktail menu trend that was championed by

bartending legend, Don the Beachcomber, (he was of such high repute that his status was of that usually afforded only to movie stars) and, to a lesser degree, his pupil, Trader Vic. Zombies, Mai Tais and Scorpions were all to become drinks that not only stood the test of time but also remind people of sun-kissed beaches and tropical holidays.

However, by the 1960s, cocktail consumption was going nowhere. Free love, drug culture and the perceived stuffiness of cocktail lounges meant that cocktails didn't really move forward. And so to the next decade.... Cocktails went the same way that most things went in the 1970s – take your pick from the Tequila Sunrise to the Piña Colada, the 1970s did to the cocktail what, well, the 1970s did to everything else.

The 1980s didn't help the situation at all, nor did the Thatcher and Reagan mentality. Spirits (and bank balances) were high, but never more so than when it came to the potency of cocktails. For some reason, bartenders seemed to do their damnedest to stifle the creativity of cocktail making by performing such demeaning feats as stuffing candy bars and jelly beans into bottles of vodka and selling them at dirt cheap prices.

Who knows what lies in store for the cocktail in the next millennium? One thing's for certain, however: there is a cocktail for everyone and for every occasion. It's just down to you to experiment with some recipes and find the right one for you.

equipment

For the aspiring home bartender, getting the right equipment can be as important as the taste of the final drink itself. You will probably find that you already have most of what you need to make cocktails in your own kitchen. But if you want to create the right atmosphere for your guests and mix cocktails with a little more flair, it's worth getting a few accessories.

JIGGER The jigger is an essential piece of equipment for making cocktails. Jiggers come in a variety of sizes, from the single shot of 25 ml/1 oz. to 150 ml/6 oz. for a small glass of wine. If you can find the double jigger (one end holds 25 ml/1 oz., the other 50 ml/2 oz.) you are starting off on the right foot. Your common or garden teaspoon will also be useful for measuring smaller quantities.

SHAKER The item most synonymous with the world of the 'spiritual advisor' is the cocktail shaker. While there are only two basic types of shaker – the three-piece (or deco) shaker and the modern-day professional bartender's (MPB) favourite, the Boston shaker – they can come in many shapes and sizes from the rather apt fire extinguishers to the more abstract lighthouses and penguins. The three-piece (so named as it comes in three pieces – the can, the strainer and the lid) is suitable for home creations and for the more elegant world of the hotel bartender. Bartenders prefer the Boston shaker, purely for ergonomic reasons. Its two separate parts (the mixing glass and the can) allow the bartender more volume and yield greater results in the shake.

STRAINER Whenever possible, strain your concoction over fresh ice as the ice you have used in your shaker will already have started to dilute. If the Boston is your tool of choice, you will need something to strain the liquid out while keeping the ice in. There are two types of strainer – the Hawthorn strainer will sit happily over the metal part of the shaker, while the Julep fits comfortably in the mixing glass.

BARSPOON and MUDDLER The barspoon (or Bonzer) is the Swiss army knife of the cocktail world. This tool comes in a number of styles; the long, spiral stemmed, flat-ended spoon is the most versatile. As well as all the obvious uses for a spoon (measuring and stirring), the spiral stem and flat end is perfect for creating layered drinks (see page 17). The flat end can also be used for gentle muddling (dissolving powders into liquid, for example). If more labour-intensive muddling is needed, you may want a more user-friendly piece of equipment. The muddler and the imaginatively titled 'wood' or 'stick' are more ergonomic and won't cause you as much discomfort as the Bonzer.

POURER Though not essential to the home bar, one of the tools that the MPB finds indispensable is the pourer (a thin stainless steel spout mounted on a tapered plastic bung). This piece of equipment lets us pour a liquid at a regulated rate. MPBs count to a fixed number when pouring a liquor or liqueur through a pourer, so a jigger isn't necessary. Different liquors will pour at different speeds, however, depending on the amount of sugar in the liquids.

STRAWS For those of you starting off in the world of cocktails, a straw is an essential tool. In much the same way that a chef will always taste a sauce before serving it, you will need a method to hygienically test the balance of your drink. Dip a straw into the beverage in question and once submerged, place your finger over the top end to create a vacuum. Take the straw from the drink and suck the liquid from the straw – this small amount will be enough for you to determine whether your drink needs more sweetening or souring agent. This is called the pipette method, and is used by bartenders all over the world when creating new drinks.

BLENDER Although the blender is an essential tool for any bar, be aware that it can turn cocktails into watery mush at the flick of a switch. And besides, it's very difficult to entertain your guests over the noise of a blender at full speed. A prosaic kitchen blender should suffice. Try to use crushed ice rather than cubes in the blender – it will add years to the life of its blades.

ICE Ice is another essential (and often overlooked) tool of every bartender. If you are making ice at home, make sure you use spring rather than tap water to avoid having chlorinated ice cubes. There are three different types of ice: cubed, crushed and shaved. Cubed ice will melt (and therefore add dilution) at a much slower rate but will also chill a cocktail less effectively than crushed or shaved ice. Drinks using crushed ice have risen in popularity recently, owing mostly to the arrival on the cocktail scene of concoctions like the Caipirinha and the Mojito. Shaved ice is mostly used in drinks that might require a little dilution to make them more palatable (remember, water is an important ingredient in a great many mixed drinks) and where they need to be absolutely as cold as possible.

glassware

Contrary to popular belief, you do not need to have an exhaustive range of glasses to create great cocktails. The glasses below should cover your needs.

The SHOT GLASS is fairly self-explanatory; it usually holds either a single or a double shot and is used for serving shots and shooters. It can also be used as a jigger should you lose yours (a common occurrence even for the pros).

The OLD-FASHIONED GLASS (also known as the ROCKS GLASS or TUMBLER) is used for drinks that are served on the rocks (short drinks over ice). It should have a capacity of about 350 ml/12 oz. and can also house drinks like whisky and soda.

The HIGHBALL GLASS is a tall thin glass used for long cocktails and also for serving liquors with mixers. Anything over 350 ml/ 12 oz. should suffice.

The HEATPROOF GLASS is for serving hot drinks, so take your pick from the wine-glass-shaped Irish coffee glass to the type of tall glass in which you might be served a café latte in a restaurant.

You will need a WINE GLASS and a CHAMPAGNE FLUTE of some shape. As there is no real restriction on these, you can be as ornate as you choose.

A MARTINI GLASS is a must for any aspiring mixologist. The longer the stem, the more ornate. Martini glasses holding 150–200 ml/ 5–7 oz. should suffice for drinks that are served straight up.

A MARGARITA COUPETTE is useful but not essential. This glass is also called the Marie Antoinette (so named as it is rumoured the glass was shaped around the curve of her breast).

The HURRICANE GLASS is a multi-purpose glass, which comes in a number of different shapes and sizes. Generally seen as a glass that holds punches and frozen drinks, it is also known as the TULIP.

glassware 15

techniques

There are six basic techniques behind the creation of a cocktail – layering, building, stirring, muddling, shaking and blending. When creating a mixed drink, it is important to remember two of the principles of cocktail making – first, to marry the flavours of the ingredients and secondly, to chill the ingredients. These simple principles can be applied to virtually any mixed drink. The only exception to this rule is the layered drink.

SHAKING (1) Drinks that contain heavy ingredients need an aggressive method of mixing and chilling. You will find that a good, sharp shake will bring life to 'heavy' ingredients. When shaking a cocktail there are a few things to remember. Whether you are using a three-piece shaker or a Boston, make sure you have one hand at each end of the shaker and shake vertically, making sure the ice and liquid travel the full distance of the shaker. When using a Boston, the cocktail should always be made in the mixing glass, so those who are enjoying the spectacle of your labour can see what is going into the drink (it's not that complex guys, honestly!). Add as much ice to the mixing glass as possible and attach the can squarely over the top to create a vacuum. Shake sharply until the outside of the stainless steel part of the shaker frosts over. When creating a shaken cocktail, always pour from the metal part of the shaker (it has a lip to stop the liquid dribbling down the outside of the vessel and the metal will help to sustain the temperature of the drink).

POUSSE CAFE or **LAYERING (2)** Literally meaning 'push coffee', the Pousse Café was invented by the French and was served as an accompaniment to coffee, the two being sipped alternately. To layer a cocktail, there are a couple of rules that need to be adhered to. First, choose liquors that will look dramatic when layered on top of one another in the glass. There isn't much point in layering liquids if they are of the same colour. Secondly, layer each liquid in order of density – this means adding the heaviest spirits first as they will sit at the bottom of the glass. The lower the alcohol content in a liquor and the greater the sugar level, the denser the liquid will be. Therefore, the liquor or liqueur that is the sweetest and has the lowest proof (percentage of alcohol) should be poured into the glass first. The higher the proof and the lower the sugar content, the lighter the spirit is. Be warned – this technique requires a steady hand. Pour your first ingredient into the shot glass. Pour your second down the spiral stem of a bar-spoon with the flat end resting on the surface of the liquid below.

BUILDING (3) Building is the term used to describe pouring a drink into a glass, one ingredient after another. It is the technique you would use to make a tall drink such as a gin and tonic or a Screwdriver. Once 'built' in the glass, the mixture may need a quick stir with a barspoon or the addition of a swizzle stick. When building a drink, always add as much ice to the glass as possible.

STIRRING (4) When the ingredients in a drink are all alcoholic, the best method of mixing and chilling them is stirring. Stirred drinks should always be made in the mixing glass. If you have the time, chill the glass first by adding ice and stirring gently with a barspoon (make sure any dilution is discarded before the alcohol is added), or place the glass in the freezer for an hour prior to making the drink. When stirring a drink, place your spoon in the glass and gently stir the ice in a continuous manner. Add all the ingredients and continue stirring until the liquid is as cold as it can be (about 32°F). You may find it easier to strain the drink from the mixing glass using a Julep strainer.

MUDDLING (5) Muddling a drink may require the use of a barspoon, a muddler or a stick, depending on the intensity of the muddling. As opposed to stirring, a muddled drink will invariably incorporate the intentional dilution of ice at some stage. Whether releasing the flavour or aroma of an herb (such as mint in the Mojito), dissolving powder into a liquid (such as sugar into the Old Fashioned), or extracting the juices of a fruit (such as fresh limes in a Caipirinha), the tool may change but the method is the same.

BLENDING You would usually be called upon to blend a drink when its ingredients involve heavy dairy products (as in the Piña Colada) or fresh fruit and frozen variations on classic drinks (Strawberry Daiquiri or frozen margaritas). Always use ready-crushed ice in a blender, and blend for about 20 seconds. When adding the crushed ice, the key phrase is 'less is more'. Add too much ice and the drink becomes solid in constitution (and then what do you have to do? That's right, add more liquid!). Add a little ice at a time though, and you can achieve the perfect thickness. Blending a cocktail will invariably produce an ultra cold, thirst-quenching cocktail. Since the ice is crushed, the drink will dilute or separate quite quickly though. Be warned, no one likes a slushy cocktail!

FLAMING Although not strictly a method of cocktail creation, this is a flamboyant means of adding a little theatre to the cocktail occasion. A liquid has to be over 40% alcohol to ignite and even then it's often difficult to get the flame to catch. A simple way to overcome this problem is to warm the glass with hot water first. However, with very high alcohol spirits this will not be necessary. Be careful though, these spirits can often react quite aggressively and on no occasion should you ever try to ignite them from the bottle!

martinis

classic martini

This is how to make a 'standard martini' for anyone who asked for one. While the pouring or building technique (see page 18) is faster and the resultant drink stronger (less dilute), stirring the cocktail is a more authentic method and the original labour of love for any true bartender.

a dash of vermouth (Noilly Prat or Martini Extra Dry)
75 ml/3 oz. freezing gin or vodka
an olive or a lemon twist, to garnish

Serves 1

Add both the ingredients to a mixing glass filled with ice and stir. Strain into a frosted martini glass and garnish with an olive or a twist of lemon.

smoky martini

Try using a very smoky malt, such as Talisker, or a peated one, such as Laphroaig, for interesting results.

50 ml/2 oz. gin
a dash of dry vermouth
a dash of whisky
a lemon zest, to garnish

Serves 1

Add all the ingredients to a shaker filled with ice. Shake sharply and strain into a chilled martini glass with a lemon-zested rim.

gibson

The leading theory behind the origin of this classic martini is that it was first made at the beginning of the 20th century for Charles Gibson, a famous illustrator, at the Players Club in New York. Whatever its roots, this classic drink has truly withstood the test of time.

a dash of vermouth (Noilly Prat or Martini Extra Dry)

75 ml/3 oz. freezing gin or vodka

pearl onions, to garnish

Serves 1

Add both the ingredients to a mixing glass filled with ice and stir. Strain into a frosted martini glass and garnish with a pearl onion or two.

churchill martini

Winston Churchill, like many of his contemporaries, would search for ways to prevent his beloved martini being sabotaged by the inclusion of too much vermouth. So, whereas some just aromatize their martini with vermouth and others marinade their olives in vermouth, Churchill would merely look at the bottle when fixing himself a martini!

(ALSO KNOWN AS THE NAKED MARTINI)

50 ml/2 oz. gin
1 bottle dry vermouth
a green olive, to garnish

Serves 1

Using a mixing glass, chill a large shot of gin over ice and pour into a frosted martini glass. (An easier method is to keep a bottle of gin in the freezer.) Pass a bottle of vermouth over the drink, ensuring that the sun shines through the liquid onto the martini! Garnish with a green olive.

Named by James Bond in the film *Casino Royale* – Bond christened the drink he devised after his Bond girl *de-jour* Vesper Lynd. A shaken, medium-dry concoction.

vesper

60 ml/2½ oz. gin
4 teaspoons vodka
2 teaspoons Kina Lillet (French vermouth)
a long lemon zest, to garnish

Serves 1

Add all the ingredients to a shaker filled with ice. Shake and strain into a frosted martini glass. Garnish with a lemon zest and serve.

montgomery

This martini is named after Field Marshall Montgomery, a veteran of the Second World War. Considering 'Monty' fought in the North African Desert, it's surprising that he didn't prefer something less dry!

1 part vermouth
15 parts gin or vodka
an olive or a lemon zest, to garnish

Add all the ingredients to a mixing glass filled with ice and stir. Strain into a frosted martini or rocks glass and garnish with an olive or a lemon zest.

Serves 1

horse's

This recipe stems from the days when gin and vodka were considered medicinal. The ginger would have been added not only to flavour the elixir, but also to act as a herbal remedy to cure most ills.

12.5 ml/½ oz. ginger liqueur
50 ml/2 oz. vodka
a whole lemon zest, to garnish

Serves 1

Add both the ingredients to a shaker filled with ice. Shake sharply and strain into a frosted martini glass. Garnish with a whole lemon zest.

martinez

The Martinez is believed to be the first documented martini, dating back as far as 1849 when it was mixed for a miner who had just struck gold in the town of Martinez, California. Its sweet flavours were geared to appeal to the taste buds of the time and the availability of certain spirits.

50 ml/2 oz. **Old Tom gin**
12.5 ml/½ oz. **sweet vermouth**
a dash of **orange bitters**
a dash of **maraschino**
a **lemon twist**, to garnish

Serves 1

Add all the ingredients to a shaker filled with ice. Shake and strain into a frosted martini glass. Garnish and serve.

dirty martini

This martini is also known as the FDR after the man who called an end to Prohibition in the 1920s. Fittingly, the great president was an accomplished bartender who loved nothing more than flourishing his shaker for any head of state with a like mind or a dry palate.

a dash of vermouth (Noilly Prat or Martini Extra Dry)

75 ml/3 oz. freezing gin or vodka

a large dash of brine from the olive or onion jar

an olive, a lemon twist or a pearl onion, to garnish

Serves 1

Add all the ingredients to a shaker filled with ice. Shake sharply and strain into a frosted martini glass. Garnish with an olive, a twist of lemon or a pearl onion.

the ultimate martini

Every martini should be made using the very finest components. Make this martini the 'ultimate' by choosing from the exceptional quality spirits now available.

a drop of Vya dry vermouth

50 ml/2 oz. freezing ultra premium gin or vodka

a lemon twist or an olive, to garnish

Serves 1

Rinse a frosted martini glass with the vermouth and discard. Add the spirit and garnish with a twist of lemon or an olive.

raspberry martini

This martini should be quite thick in consistency, so if you aren't using pre-made purée, use a good handful of raspberries to ensure it flows down your neck like treacle.

50 ml/2 oz. vodka
a dash of framboise
a dash of orange bitters
12.5 ml/½ oz. raspberry purée
2 fresh raspberries, to garnish

Serves 1

Add all the ingredients to a shaker filled with ice. Shake sharply and strain into a frosted martini glass. Garnish with two fresh raspberries.

cherry martini

This martini can also be made using the juice from canned cherries – it may not sound as nice on paper but wait until you taste it. For a delicious variation, try using the juice from canned lychees – another winner!

3 pitted fresh cherries
50 ml/2 oz. vodka
50 ml/2 oz. thick cherry juice
a dash of cherry schnapps

Serves 1

Crush the cherries in a shaker. Add ice and the remaining ingredients, shake sharply and strain through a sieve into a frosted martini glass.

This fruit martini is certainly not for the faint-hearted. Unlike a lot of the fruit martinis whose sweetness belies their strength, this one pulls no punches.

**50 ml/2 oz. vodka
a dash of Poire William eau de vie
a thin pear slice, to garnish**

serves 1

pear martini

Add all the ingredients to a shaker filled with ice. Shake and strain through a sieve into a frosted martini glass. Garnish with a thin slice of pear.

Another old favourite, the citrus needs to be shaken hard to take the edge off the lemon. Try substituting lime for lemon for a slightly more tart variation.

citrus martini

Add all the ingredients to a shaker filled with ice. Shake sharply and strain into a frosted martini glass. Garnish with a lemon zest.

**50 ml/2 oz. Cytrynowka vodka
25 ml/1 oz. fresh lemon juice
25 ml/1 oz. Cointreau
a dash of sugar syrup
a lemon zest, to garnish**

serves 1

As this is one of the subtler of the fruit martinis, care must be taken to ensure the pomegranate is ripe. Try to avoid getting any of the fruit's bitter pith in the drink, as this would destroy its delicate balance.

pomegranate martini

1 pomegranate
50 ml/2 oz. vodka
a dash of sugar syrup
pomegranate seeds, to garnish

serves 1

Spoon the pomegranate 'flesh' into a shaker and crush, using a muddler or the flat end of a barspoon. Add ice to the shaker with the remaining ingredients. Shake sharply and strain through a sieve into a frosted martini glass. Garnish with a few pomegranate seeds.

The bitterness of Zubrowka with the potent sweetness of Krupnik combine with the crispness of apple juice to create a beguiling depth of taste.

polish martini

25 ml/1 oz. Zubrowka vodka

25 ml/1 oz. Krupnik vodka

25 ml/1 oz. fresh apple juice

serves 1

Add all the ingredients to a mixing glass filled with ice and stir. Strain into a chilled martini glass.

french martini

The French martini is great for parties as it is light and creamy, and simple to make in bulk. Shake this one hard when preparing it and you will be rewarded with a thick white froth on the surface of the drink.

50 ml/2 oz. vodka

a large dash of Chambord (or crème de mure)

75 ml/3 oz. fresh pineapple juice

Add all the ingredients to a shaker filled with ice. Shake sharply and strain into a frosted martini glass.

serves 1

The Sake Martini uses the heady combination of gin, vodka and sake, which might not sound very tempting but it's definitely worth having a try next time you order that takeaway sushi!

sake martini

Add all the ingredients to a mixing glass filled with ice. Stir the mixture until thoroughly chilled and strain into a frosted martini glass. Garnish with an olive or a slice of cucumber.

25 ml/1 oz. sake
25 ml/1 oz. vodka
a dash of gin
olive or a cucumber
slice, to garnish

serves 1

Cachaça works amazingly well when mixed with lime and sugar in a Caipirinha (see page 118), so it stands to reason that it can work well on its own.

azure martini

Pound the apple in the bottom of a shaker to release the flavour. Add crushed ice and the remaining ingredients, shake and strain through a sieve into a frosted martini glass.

½ **apple**
50 ml/2 oz. **cachaça**
12.5 ml/½ oz. **canella liqueur**
a dash of fresh lime or lemon juice
a dash of sugar syrup

serves 1

breakfast martini

Invented by Salvatore Calabrese at The Library Bar at The Lanesborough Hotel, London. If you fancy something a little more tangy, try replacing the orange marmalade with lime marmalade.

50 ml/2 oz. gin
2 teaspoons Cointreau
a dash of fresh lemon juice
2 barspoons orange marmalade

serves 1

Add all the ingredients to a shaker filled with ice. Shake sharply and strain into a chilled martini glass.

applejack

Taken from recipes using American apple brandy, this concoction relies heavily on the addition of Manzana apple liqueur, a green apple liqueur that lends a bitter-sweet quality to the martini.

25 ml/1 oz. vodka
25 ml/1 oz. Manzana apple liqueur
4 teaspoons Calvados
a thin apple slice, to garnish

serves 1

Add all the ingredients to a mixing glass filled with ice, stir until the glass appears frosted then strain into a frosted martini glass. Garnish with a thin slice of apple.

blood martini

A bittersweet concoction that needs to be delicately balanced. The lime and the Campari provide the bitterness, while the sweet element comes in the form of the raspberry liqueur. Taste the drink before and after adding the orange zest – what a difference!

50 ml/2 oz. vodka
1 tablespoon Campari
2 teaspoons framboise
1 teaspoon fresh lime juice
2 tablespoons cranberry juice
a dash of Cointreau
a flaming orange zest, to garnish

serves 1

Add all the ingredients to a shaker filled with ice. Shake sharply and strain into a frosted martini glass. Garnish with a flaming orange zest (see page 86).

legend

50 ml/2 oz. vodka
25 ml/1 oz. crème de mure
25 ml/1 oz. fresh lime juice
a dash of sugar syrup

serves 1

Invented in London in the late 1980s, this recipe has to be followed closely as too much of any of the ingredients can result in an unpalatable cocktail. Make sure you taste each concoction before you serve it.

Add all the ingredients to a shaker filled with ice. Shake sharply and strain into a frosted martini glass.

hazelnut martini

This martini has proved popular with men and women alike. A strong, clear chocolate martini with an undercurrent of hazelnut thanks to the Frangelico, it is perfect after dinner with a coffee – a dessert and a nightcap rolled into one.

50 ml/2 oz. vodka
4 teaspoons white crème de cacao
2 teaspoons Frangelico
grated nutmeg, for the glass

Add all the ingredients to a shaker filled with ice. Shake and strain into a frosted martini glass rimmed with grated nutmeg.

serves 1

This martini is a snip to prepare as it involves no fresh fruit. Strong and sweet, it should appeal to a wide range of tastes.

pontberry martini

50 ml/2 oz. vodka
75 ml/3 oz. cranberry juice
a large dash of crème de mure

serves 1

Add all the ingredients to a shaker filled with ice. Shake, strain into a frosted martini glass and serve.

If you've long searched for a credible drink that includes rose water, here it is. The heaviness of the crème de cacao combines with the lightness of the flower water to create a truly Turkish delight!

turkish chocolate

50 ml/2 oz. vodka
2 teaspoons white crème de cacao
2 dashes of rose water
cocoa powder, for the glass

serves 1

Add all the ingredients to a shaker filled with ice. Shake and strain into a frosted martini glass rimmed with cocoa powder.

chocatini

25 g/1 oz. dark chocolate
50 ml/2 oz. vodka
3 tablespoons crème de cacao

serves 1

Melt the chocolate by placing it in a heatproof bowl set over a saucepan of just-simmering water (do not let the bowl touch the water). Stir until melted.

Transfer the chocolate to a plate. Take a martini glass and carefully dip the rim into the melted chocolate to give a thin line of chocolate. Invert and put in the fridge to set for 20 minutes.

Add the vodka and crème de cacao to a shaker filled with ice. Shake vigorously but briefly and strain into the chilled, chocolate-rimmed glass. Serve immediately.

a dash of Parfait
Amour
50 ml/2 oz. chilled
Bombay Sapphire gin
fresh blueberries, to
garnish

serves 1

A couple of drops of Parfait Amour,
a beautifully named orange curaçao
flavoured with violets, combined with
well-chilled Bombay Sapphire gin produces
a magnificent cocktail.

sapphire martini

Gently pour the Parfait Amour into a frosted
martini glass. Pour the gin (which should have
been in the freezer for at least 1 hour) over a
barspoon, so that it sits over the liqueur. Garnish
with blueberries on a cocktail stick.

4 fresh blackcurrants
50 ml/2 oz. Zubrowka vodka
4 teaspoons Chambord or
crème de mure
12.5 ml/½ oz. fresh lime juice
a dash of sugar syrup
a fresh blueberry, to garnish

serves 1

black bison

The central ingredient to this mix is
Zubrowka, a vodka that tastes of freshly
cut hay, and lends a distinct quality to any
cocktail. Combine this with Chambord and
you have a truly memorable union!

Muddle the blackcurrants in a shaker. Add the
remaining ingredients to the shaker with ice.
Shake sharply and strain into a frosted martini
glass. Garnish with a blueberry.

A cocktail that is as sinister and mysterious as the name suggests. Try varying the amount of black Sambuca (one of the most underused cocktail ingredients I know) for a darker, more threatening result.

gotham

60 ml/2½ oz. frozen Stolichnaya vodka

a dash of black Sambuca

serves 1

Pour the vodka into a frosted martini glass, gently add the Sambuca. Serve.

black dog

For those who love the idea of a martini but refuse to be budged from drinking rum-based cocktails, the Black Dog is the answer.

50 ml/2 oz. light rum

a dash of dry vermouth

a black olive, to garnish

serves 1

Add both the ingredients to a mixing glass filled with ice and stir rhythmically and gently. Once the mixture is thoroughly chilled, strain into a frosted martini glass and garnish with a black olive.

thunderer

This cocktail smells almost perfumed. A hint of Parfait Amour and a tease of crème de cassis is all this drink needs to achieve its flowery, distinctive taste.

2 drops of Parfait Amour
2 drops of crème de cassis
60 ml/2½ oz. frozen vodka
2 fresh blueberries, to garnish

serves 1

Pour the Parfait Amour and cassis into a frosted martini glass. Add the frozen vodka and garnish with two blueberries.

joe average

Despite its name, there is nothing average about this drink. Nor should the Pimm's in the recipe fool you – this is not a drink to be taken lightly!

60 ml/2½ oz. Stolichnaya vodka
a dash of Pimm's No. 1
a thin cucumber slice and a lemon zest, to garnish

serves 1

Add both the ingredients to a mixing glass filled with ice, stir until the glass appears frosted then strain into a frosted martini glass. Garnish with a thin slice of cucumber and a lemon zest.

tequilini

Chilled to perfection and softened by the vermouth, this cocktail is a great way to serve an aged tequila.

a dash of dry vermouth
50 ml/2 oz. premium añejo tequila
a lime zest, to garnish

serves 1

Add a dash of vermouth to a mixing glass filled with ice. Stir gently then discard any dilution. Add the tequila and stir again for fifteen seconds. Strain the mixture into a frosted martini glass and garnish with a lime zest.

red star

The Red Star is a delicate drink.
Ensure the glass is well frosted
to highlight the hint of aniseed
taken from the seed of this
Chinese plant.

**15 ml/¾ oz. star anise-infused dry
vermouth (see below)**
50 ml/2 oz. vodka
a star anise, to garnish

serves 1

Star anise-infused dry vermouth:
Infuse four star anises in a small
bottle of Noilly Prat vermouth for
two days.

Add the infused dry vermouth and
the vodka to a mixing glass filled
with ice and stir until the glass is
frosted. Strain into a frosted martini
glass and garnish with a star anise.

cajun martini

A word of warning, this drink must be monitored while it is infusing. Habañero chillies are incredibly strong and should be treated with respect. A glass of milk will neutralize the effect if you overdo it!

60 ml/2½ oz. habañero-infused vodka (see below)
½ pitted habañero chilli, to garnish (don't eat it!)

serves 1

Habañero-infused vodka: Place three habañero chillies (with seeds) into a bottle of vodka and leave until they start to lose their colour – the more translucent the chillies become, the more flavour has been absorbed into the vodka. (This will take a few days.)

Add the infused vodka to a mixing glass filled with ice and stir until the glass is frosted. Strain into a frosted martini glass and garnish with a habañero chilli.

hibiscus

It's always worth experimenting with the Hibiscus before you serve it to your guests, as the concentration of the juice can vary – overdo the hibiscus if in doubt.

50 ml/2 oz. hibiscus cordial (see below)
25 ml/1 oz. vodka
a dash of fresh lime juice
a dash of framboise liqueur
a hibiscus flower or petal, to garnish

serves 1

Hibiscus cordial: Dissolve 500 g/2½ cups sugar and 100 g/3½ oz. hibiscus flowers (dried if out of season) in 2 litres/8 cups water on a low heat. Once the liquid turns a deep red, strain and leave to cool.

Add the hibiscus cordial and the remaining ingredients to a shaker filled with ice. Shake sharply and strain into a frosted martini glass. Garnish with a hibiscus flower.

The Vodkatini has all but overtaken the original gin martini in popularity. As with the gin martini, there are four important things to consider when it comes to making a Vodkatini: the quantity of vermouth, to shake or stir, straight up or on the rocks and lastly, an olive or a twist.

vodkatini

a dash of dry vermouth
50 ml/2 oz. vodka
a pitted olive or a lemon zest, to garnish

serves 1

Fill a mixing glass with ice and stir with a barspoon until the glass is chilled. Tip the water out and top with ice. Add a dash of dry vermouth and continue stirring. Strain the liquid away and top with ice. Add the vodka and stir in a continuous circular motion until the vodka is thoroughly chilled (taking care not to chip the ice and dilute the vodka). Strain into a frosted martini glass and garnish with either a pitted olive or a lemon zest.

pink gin

Pink Gin is a thoroughly English cocktail which, although it originated as a medicinal potion in the British navy, became one of the smartest drinks in 1940s' London.

2 dashes of Angostura bitters
50 ml/2 oz. chilled gin

serves 1

Rinse a frosted sherry or martini glass with Angostura bitters, add chilled gin and serve.

A great 'litmus' test for a bartender's capability – too much lime and the drink turns sickly, not enough and the drink is too strong. This one needs to be shaken hard to ensure a sharp freezing zestiness.

gin gimlet

50 ml/2 oz. gin
25 ml/1 oz. lime cordial

Add both the ingredients to a shaker filled with ice. Shake very sharply and strain into a frosted martini glass.

serves 1

negroni

The Negroni packs a powerful punch but still makes an elegant aperitif. For a drier variation, add a little more dry gin, but if a fruitier cocktail is more to your taste, wipe some orange zest around the top of the glass and add some to the drink.

25 ml/1 oz. Campari
25 ml/1 oz. sweet vermouth
25 ml/1 oz. gin
an orange zest, to garnish

serves 1

Build all the ingredients into a rocks glass filled with ice, garnish with an orange zest and stir.

If you enjoy the lingering flavour of pastis, try adding Pernod to the drink rather than just rinsing the glass with it.

new orleans sazarac

25 ml/1 oz. Pernod
1 sugar cube
dashes of Angostura bitters
50 ml/2 oz. bourbon

serves 1

Rinse an old-fashioned glass with Pernod then discard the Pernod. Put the sugar in the glass, saturate with Angostura bitters, then add ice cubes and the bourbon and serve.

sidecar

50 ml/2 oz. brandy
4 teaspoons fresh lemon juice
4 teaspoons Cointreau
sugar, for the glass

serves 1

The Sidecar, like many of the classic cocktails created in the 1920s, is attributed to the inventive genius of Harry McElhone, who founded Harry's New York Bar in Paris. It is said to have been created in honour of an eccentric military man who would roll up outside the bar in the sidecar of his chauffeur-driven motorcycle.

Shake all the ingredients in a shaker filled with ice. Strain into a frosted martini glass rimmed with sugar.

The classic Old Fashioned is a drink that demands attention from its maker. Despite the relative simplicity of its ingredients, neglect the detail of the preparation at your peril. The delicate mix of sugar and orange zest will bring to life whichever bourbon you choose to use.

old fashioned

1 white sugar cube
2 dashes of orange bitters
50 ml/2 oz. bourbon
a strip of orange zest

serves 1

Place the sugar cube soaked with orange bitters into a rocks glass, muddle the mixture with a barspoon and add a dash of bourbon and a couple of ice cubes. Keep adding ice and bourbon and keep muddling until the full 50 ml/2 oz. has been added to the glass (ensuring the sugar has dissolved). Rim the glass with a zest of orange and drop it into the glass.

sparkling cocktails

champagne cocktail

This cocktail has truly stood the test of time, being as popular now as when it was sipped by stars of the silver screen in the 1940s. It's a simple and delicious cocktail, which epitomizes the elegance and sophistication of that era and still lends the same touch of urbanity (one hopes!) to those who drink it today.

1 white sugar cube
2 dashes of Angostura bitters
25 ml/1 oz. brandy
dry champagne, to top up

serves 1

Place the sugar cube in a champagne flute and moisten with Angostura bitters. Add the brandy, stir then gently pour in the champagne and serve.

ginger champagne

The ginger combines conspiratorially with the champagne to create a cocktail that is delicate yet different enough to appease even the most sophisticated cocktail drinker.

2 thin fresh ginger slices
25 ml/1 oz. vodka
champagne, to top up

serves 1

Put the ginger in a shaker and press with a barspoon or muddler to release the flavour. Add ice and the vodka, shake and strain into a champagne flute. Top with champagne and serve.

bellini

The Bellini originated in Harry's Bar in Venice in the early 1940s. Although there are many variations on this recipe, there is one golden rule for the perfect Bellini – always use fresh, ripe peaches to make the peach juice.

½ fresh peach, skinned
12.5 ml/½ oz. crème de pêche
a dash of peach bitters (optional)
champagne, to top up
a peach ball, to garnish

serves 1

Purée the peach in a blender and add to a champagne flute. Pour in the crème de pêche and the peach bitters, and gently top up with champagne, stirring carefully and continuously. Garnish with a peach ball in the bottom of the glass, then serve.

rossini

A great variation on the Bellini, the Rossini is spiced up with a little Chambord and a dash of orange bitters – two of a bartender's favourite cocktail ingredients.

1 tablespoon raspberry purée
1 teaspoon Chambord
2 dashes of orange bitters
champagne, to top up

serves 1

Add the purée, Chambord and bitters to a champagne flute and top gently with champagne. Stir gently and serve.

blood orange & campari mimosa

Mimosa or Buck's Fizz is a standard offering at brunch gatherings, but this one is different. The Campari and blood orange make it a little bitter, and this really whets the appetite. If anyone needs his or hers sweetened – not everyone gets the bitter thing – add a dash of agave syrup or honey and serve with a cocktail stirrer.

500 ml/2 cups pure blood orange juice
4 dashes of Campari
750-ml bottle sparkling white wine, chilled

serves 4

Divide the blood orange juice between four champagne flutes. Add a dash of Campari to each one, then top up with the sparkling wine.

champagne julep

This cocktail works with all types of champagne or sparkling wine. If you have a bottle of bubbly that has been open for a while and lost a bit of its fizz, don't worry, the sugar in the recipe will revitalize it.

5 fresh mint sprigs, plus 1 to garnish
1 tablespoon sugar syrup
a dash of fresh lime juice
champagne, to top up

serves 1

Muddle the mint, sugar syrup and lime juice together in a highball glass. Add crushed ice and the champagne gently and stir. Garnish with a sprig of mint and serve.

black velvet

There is probably no drink in the world that looks more tempting and drinkable than a Black Velvet. Pour this drink gently into the glass to allow for the somewhat unpredictable nature of both the Guinness and the champagne.

½ glass Guinness
champagne, to top up

serves 1

Half-fill a champagne flute with Guinness, gently top with champagne and serve.

kir royale

After a shaky start, the Kir Royale is now the epitome of chic sophistication (unless of course you prefer yours looking and tasting like alcoholic Ribena!). It started life as the Kir (a variation using acidic white wine instead of champagne) and was called *rince cochon* ('pig rinse'!). Luckily, the wine became less sharp and the drink adopted a more appropriate mantle!

a dash of crème de cassis

champagne, to top up

serves 1

Add a small dash of crème de cassis to a champagne flute and gently top with champagne. Stir gently and serve.

french 75

Named after the big artillery gun that terrorized the Germans during the First World War, rattling off rounds at a rate of 30 per minute. The popular variation on this drink was to mix Cognac with the champagne, which would make sense since they were fighting in France!

4 teaspoons gin
2 teaspoons fresh lemon juice
1 barspoon sugar syrup
champagne, to top up
a lemon zest, to garnish

serves 1

Add the gin, lemon juice and sugar syrup to a shaker filled with ice. Shake and strain into a champagne flute. Top with champagne and garnish with a long strip of lemon zest.

metropolis

25 ml/1 oz. vodka
25 ml/1 oz. crème de framboise
champagne, to top up

serves 1

The Metropolis was a logical creation since the champagne and berry-flavoured liqueur combination was such an obvious success in the Kir Royale (see page 73). Adding vodka gave a kick to that same seductive mix of champagne and fruit flavours.

Add the vodka and crème de framboise to a shaker filled with ice. Shake and strain into a martini glass. Top with champagne and serve.

The James Bond is a variation on the Champagne Cocktail (see page 66), using vodka instead of the more traditional brandy. The naming of this cocktail is a mystery to me since the eponymous spy liked his drinks shaken not stirred, as in this cocktail.

james bond

1 white sugar cube
2 dashes of Angostura bitters
25 ml/1 oz. vodka
champagne, to top up

serves 1

Place the sugar cube in a champagne flute and moisten with Angostura bitters. Add the vodka and top with champagne.

The fruity melody of flavours combines with the champagne to make this drink the perfect cure for the blues.

apricot royale

40 ml/1¾ oz. apricot brandy
1 tablespoon fresh lemon juice
1 tablespoon simple syrup
a dash of peach bitters
a dash of orange bitters
champagne, to float
an apricot slice, to garnish

serves 1

Add all the ingredients, except the champagne, to a shaker filled with ice. Shake sharply and strain into a rocks glass or tumbler filled with ice. Gently layer a float of champagne over the surface of the drink. Garnish with a slice of apricot and serve.

new orleans fizz

The inclusion of rose water in the New Orleans Fizz accentuates the juniper flavour in the gin, while the dash of cream gives this very light drink a little more body.

50 ml/2 oz. gin

25 ml/1 oz. fresh lemon juice

1 barspoon white sugar or 12.5 ml/ ½ oz. sugar syrup

12.5 ml/½ oz. rose water or orange flower water

12.5 ml/½ oz. single/light cream

a dash of egg white

soda water/club soda, to top up

a lemon slice, to garnish

serves 1

Add all the ingredients, except the soda, to a shaker filled with ice. Shake vigorously and strain into a highball glass over ice. Gently add the soda, stirring with a barspoon while doing so, and garnish with a slice of lemon.

royal gin fizz

An offshoot of the original Gin Fizz, the Royal Gin Fizz has become fashionable in its own right. The substitution of the soda with champagne helps to make this cocktail special and lends it a little extra fizz – surely no harm there!

1 egg white

50 ml/2 oz. gin

25 ml/1 oz. fresh lemon juice

1 barspoon white sugar or 12.5 ml/½ oz. sugar syrup

champagne, to top up

a lemon slice, to garnish

serves 1

Add the egg white, gin, lemon juice and sugar to a shaker filled with ice. Shake vigorously and strain into a highball glass filled with ice. Top with champagne and garnish with a slice of lemon.

sloe gin fizz

You may need to play with the balance of flavours in this cocktail. Different brands of sloe gin have different concentrations of sweetness and flavour – as is the case with many liqueurs.

25 ml/1 oz. sloe gin
25 ml/1 oz. gin
4 teaspoons fresh lemon juice
2 teaspoons sugar syrup
soda water/club soda, to top up
a lemon slice, to garnish

serves 1

Add all the ingredients, except the soda, to a shaker filled with ice. Shake sharply and strain into a highball glass filled with ice. Top with soda, garnish with a slice of lemon and serve.

This fizzy little tipple is guaranteed to kick-start any big night out!

hollywood hustle

2 tablespoons citron vodka

85 ml/⅓ cup Red Bull or other fizzy energy drink

85 ml/⅓ cup champagne

Fill a chilled tumbler with crushed ice and pour over the citron vodka. Top up with the Red Bull and champagne and serve immediately.

serves 1

iced pear sparkle

1 teaspoon runny honey

2 tablespoons pear liqueur

2 tablespoons Cointreau, or other orange-flavoured liqueur

¼ pear (nashi if available), peeled and thinly sliced

champagne or sparkling white wine, to top up

serves 1

Put the honey and some ice in a shaker and gently crush with a wooden muddler. Add the pear liqueur and Cointreau, replace the lid and shake briskly but briefly.

Pour into a chilled glass, add some slices of pear and top up with champagne. Serve immediately.

cosmopolitans
& manhattans

classic cosmopolitan

The TV programme *Sex and the City* made this drink popular; its great taste has ensured it stays that way.

50 ml/2 oz. lemon vodka
4 teaspoons triple sec
4 teaspoons fresh lime juice
25 ml/1 oz. cranberry juice

serves 1

Add all the ingredients to a shaker filled with ice. Shake sharply and strain into a frosted martini glass.

ginger cosmopolitan

The mix of flaming orange zest, ginger, lime juice and lemon vodka gives this drink an incredible depth of taste.

50 ml/2 oz. lemon vodka
4 teaspoons triple sec
4 teaspoons fresh lime juice
25 ml/1 oz. cranberry juice
2 thin fresh ginger slices
a flaming orange zest, to garnish
(see page 86)

serves 1

Add all the ingredients to a shaker filled with ice. Shake sharply and strain through a sieve into a frosted martini glass. Garnish with a flaming orange zest.

metropolitan

This cocktail was one of the originals on the Met Bar menu. The blackcurrant vodka, combined with the cranberry and lime juices makes for quite a fruity concoction.

50 ml/2 oz. Absolut Kurrant vodka
25 ml/1 oz. triple sec
25 ml/1 oz. fresh lime juice
25 ml/1 oz. cranberry juice
an orange zest, to garnish

serves 1

Add all the ingredients to a shaker filled with ice. Shake sharply and strain into a frosted martini glass. Squeeze the oil from a strip of orange zest, held skin downwards and over a flame above the glass. Rub the rim with the burnt orange zest before dropping it into the glass.

rude cosmopolitan

This drink earned its name following an evening that began well enough, but descended into heated debate. The tone of the evening changed when they started to drink tequila, hence the drink's name.

50 ml/2 oz. gold tequila
4 teaspoons triple sec
25 ml/1 oz. cranberry juice
4 teaspoons fresh lime juice
a flaming orange zest, to garnish
(see opposite)

serves 1

Add all the ingredients to a shaker filled with ice. Shake and strain into a frosted martini glass. Garnish with a flaming orange zest.

bitter cosmopolitan

A cosmo should taste tangy, but using mandarin-flavoured vodka as the base here adds a level of bitterness that brings even more flavour to the drink.

50 ml/2 oz. mandarin vodka
25 ml/1 oz. fresh lime juice
25 ml/1 oz. Cointreau
50 ml/2 oz. cranberry juice
2 dashes of orange bitters
2 dashes of peach bitters

serves 1

Add all the ingredients to a shaker filled with ice. Shake sharply and strain into a frosted martini glass.

strawberry cosmopolitan

Just to prove there's a cocktail out there for everyone… If the Classic Cosmo (see page 85) is too sharp for your taste buds and the Bitter Cosmo (opposite), just too bitter, here's the one for you. Make sure that your strawberries are ripe and sweet for the best results.

3½ fresh strawberries,
plus ½ to garnish
35 ml/1½ oz. citrus vodka
25 ml/1 oz. Cointreau
1 tablespoon fresh lime juice
a dash of cranberry juice, optional

serves 1

Muddle the ripe strawberries in a shaker. Add the remaining ingredients with ice and shake sharply. Strain into a frosted martini glass and garnish with half a strawberry.

Cranberry juice lends a light, fruity, refreshing quality to this cocktail, softened by the triple sec.

cosmopolitan iced tea

2 tablespoons vodka
(vanilla-flavoured if available)
1 tablespoon triple sec
80 ml/scant ⅓ cup cranberry juice
freshly squeezed juice of ½ a lime

serves 1

Add all the ingredients to a shaker filled with ice. Shake briskly and strain into a tall glass, half-filled with ice. Serve immediately.

cosmo royale

For a fizzy spin, add a float of champagne to this great cocktail. It will happily sit on the surface if you pour it gently!

35 ml/1½ oz. lemon vodka
1 tablespoon fresh lime juice
1 tablespoon Cointreau
50 ml/2 oz. cranberry juice
champagne, to float
an orange zest, to garnish

serves 1

Add all the ingredients, except the champagne, to a shaker filled with ice. Shake sharply and strain into a frosted martini glass. Float the champagne on the surface and garnish with an orange zest.

dry manhattan

This is generally the least popular of the manhattans. The addition of dry vermouth doesn't lend the drink the warmth and reassurance that we expect from the manhattan's job description.

50 ml/2 oz. rye whiskey
25 ml/1 oz. dry vermouth
a dash of Angostura bitters
a lemon zest, to garnish

serves 1

sweet manhattan

If you are unable to find rye whiskey for this manhattan, try experimenting with bourbon instead.

50 ml/2 oz. rye whiskey
25 ml/1 oz. sweet vermouth
a dash of orange bitters
a maraschino cherry, to garnish

serves 1

perfect manhattan

'Perfect' does not refer to how well the drink is put together, it describes the perfect balance between sweet and dry.

50 ml/2 oz. rye whiskey
12.5 ml/½ oz. sweet vermouth
12.5 ml/½ oz. dry vermouth
a dash of Angostura bitters
an orange zest, to garnish

serves 1

For each of the manhattan variations, add the ingredients to a mixing glass filled with ice (first ensure all the ingredients are very cold) and stir the mixture until chilled. Strain into a frosted martini glass, add the garnish and serve.

premium manhattan

In a perfect world every drink would be made out of the finest ingredients, but the cost means it's not always possible. Every so often though, it's worth splashing out and treating yourself.

50 ml/2 oz. Knob Creek bourbon
4 teaspoons Vya dry vermouth
4 teaspoons Vya sweet vermouth
a dash of Angostura bitters
an orange zest, to garnish

serves 1

Add all the ingredients to a mixing glass filled with ice and stir gently with a barspoon. Strain into a frosted martini glass and garnish with orange zest.

añejo manhattan

This is a Perfect Manhattan (see page 93) with tequila substituting for the whiskey. Try using all sweet or all dry vermouth instead of a combination.

50 ml/2 oz. añejo tequila
4 teaspoons sweet vermouth
4 teaspoons dry vermouth
a dash of Angostura bitters
an orange zest, to garnish

serves 1

Add all the ingredients to a mixing glass filled with ice. Using a barspoon, stir in a continuous motion until the mixture is thoroughly chilled. Strain into a frosted martini glass and garnish with an orange zest.

apple manhattan

The Apple Manhattan is a grand aperitif for the more discerning palate. This delicate cocktail may also be enjoyed after an excellent dinner.

50 ml/2 oz. calvados
1 tablespoon sweet vermouth
1 tablespoon dry vermouth
an apple wedge, to garnish

serves 1

Add all the ingredients to a mixing glass filled with ice and stir gently with a barspoon. Strain into a frosted martini glass and garnish with a wedge of apple.

margaritas
& daiquiris

classic margarita

50 ml/2 oz. gold tequila

25 ml/1 oz. triple sec or Cointreau

freshly squeezed juice of ½ a lime

a lime slice, to garnish

salt, for the glass

serves 1

Beware, there are young pretenders out there who do not treat this cocktail with the respect it deserves. Premixes, poor-quality tequila, too much ice and cordial instead of fresh lemon or lime juice all contribute to an unacceptable cocktail. Don't let your margaritas be tarred by the same brush!

Add all the ingredients to a shaker filled with cracked ice. Shake sharply and strain into a frosted margarita glass rimmed with salt. Garnish with a slice of lime.

triple gold margarita

Here, a float of Goldschlager, a cinnamon-flavoured liqueur laced with real 24-carat gold pieces, adds considerably to the depth of taste of the cocktail.

50 ml/2 oz. gold tequila

2 teaspoons Cointreau

2 teaspoons Grand Marnier

4 teaspoons fresh lime juice

4 teaspoons Goldschlager

serves 1

Add all the ingredients except the Goldschlager to a shaker filled with ice. Shake sharply and strain into a frosted margarita glass. Float the Goldschlager onto the surface of the mixture and serve.

mezcal margarita

Choosing to substitute mezcal for tequila will impress any bartender. Mezcal tends to be more herbaceous and earthy on the palate – taste this drink and you'll find yourself whipped off to Mexico!

50 ml/2 oz. mezcal
2 teaspoons brandy
2 dashes of Peychaud's or Angostura bitters
4 teaspoons triple sec
4 teaspoons fresh lime juice
salt, for the glass

serves 1

Add all the ingredients to a shaker filled with ice. Shake sharply and strain into a frosted margarita glass rimmed with salt.

Patrón rightfully stands up as a tequila to be counted. But be warned, its decanter-type bottle may have upped the price on this expensive tequila. Mixed with Citronage (a premium orange liqueur), this margarita is the drink you'd choose if money were no object.

la margarita de la patron

50 ml/2 oz. Patrón Añejo tequila
35 ml/1½ oz. Citronage
4 teaspoons fresh lime juice
salt, for the glass

serves 1

Add all the ingredients to a shaker filled with ice. Shake sharply and strain into a frosted margarita glass rimmed with salt.

green iguana

The combination of melon and tequila work perfectly here. Midori (a melon-flavoured liqueur) is used in this recipe as fresh melon doesn't have the necessary sweetness to balance the drink.

2 tablespoons Sauza Hornitos tequila

25 ml/1 oz. Midori

25 ml/1 oz. fresh lime juice

25 ml/1 oz. Cointreau

a lime wedge, to garnish

serves 1

Add all the ingredients to a shaker filled with ice. Shake sharply and strain into a rocks glass.

50 ml/2 oz. gold tequila

25 ml/1 oz. fresh lime juice

1 tablespoon sugar syrup

soda water/club soda, to top up

a lime wedge, to garnish

serves 1

tequila rickey

A long tequila cooler based on one of the oldest documented cocktails, the Collins. Add plenty of lime and sugar to ensure the drink has the balance and depth of taste it deserves.

Build all the ingredients in a highball glass filled with ice. Stir gently, garnish with a wedge of lime and serve.

conmemorativo

The Conmemorativo is a variation on the margarita using a premium, aged tequila. It was a New York band, the Fun Lovin' Criminals, who, during a night at the Met Bar in London, suggested that this special tequila could be used in a cocktail just as long as it was shown respect!

1 lime, cut into 8
12.5 ml/½ oz. sugar syrup
50 ml/2 oz. Sauza Conmemorativo tequila

serves 1

Drop the lime wedges into an old-fashioned glass with sugar syrup, squeezing the lime wedges as you go, then pound well with a pestle. Fill the glass with ice and add the tequila. Stir and serve.

tres compadres

50 ml/2 oz. Sauza
Conmemorativo
tequila
4 teaspoons
Cointreau
4 teaspoons
Chambord
25 ml/1 oz. fresh
lime juice
4 teaspoons
orange juice
4 teaspoons
grapefruit juice
a lime wedge,
to garnish
salt, for the glass

serves 1

The combination of lime, orange and grapefruit juice provide the three citrus 'compadres'. Cointreau and Chambord are then added to the mix to sweeten, and lo and behold a great cocktail is born. Try serving this long (by adding more orange and grapefruit juice) for an extra refreshing cooler.

Add all the ingredients to a shaker filled with ice. Shake sharply and strain into a frosted margarita glass rimmed with salt. Garnish with a wedge of lime.

herba buena

This is a variation of the Cuban classic, the Mojito (see page 120). Pack the glass with crushed ice and this cocktail makes the perfect summer drink. Add a little extra sugar for the sweeter tooth or a little more lime for a citrus twist.

50 ml/2 oz. gold tequila
1 tablespoon fresh lime juice
1 brown rock sugar cube
5 fresh mint sprigs, plus 1 to garnish
soda water/club soda, to top up

serves 1

Muddle all the ingredients apart from the soda in a highball glass using a barspoon. Add crushed ice, muddle again and top up with the soda. Stir gently, garnish with a sprig of mint and serve with two straws.

berry margarita

50 ml/2 oz. gold tequila
4 teaspoons triple sec
4 teaspoons fresh lime juice
a dash of crème de mure
seasonal fresh berries of your
choice, plus extra to garnish

serves 1

Anything from strawberries or cranberries, to blueberries or raspberries can be used in this recipe. Choose your own combination of seasonal berries for subtle variations.

Add all the ingredients to a blender with two scoops of crushed ice and blend for 20 seconds. Pour into a margarita coupette and garnish with berries.

prickly pear margarita

The prickly pear has become *de rigueur* in cocktails and makes a great addition to the margarita.

50 ml/2 oz. silver tequila
4 teaspoons triple sec
4 teaspoons fresh lime juice
a dash of grenadine
25 ml/1 oz. prickly pear purée
a thin pear slice, to garnish

serves 1

Add all the ingredients to a shaker filled with ice. Shake sharply and strain into a frosted margarita glass. Garnish with a thin slice of pear.

mangorita

An easy cocktail to make, but tricky to get right. Mango is a powerful-tasting fruit and can overshadow the taste of tequila entirely, so take care not to add too much mango, especially if it is very ripe. Or do what I do and take care to add a little more tequila!

50 ml/2 oz. gold tequila
4 teaspoons triple sec
4 teaspoons fresh lime juice
25 ml/1 oz. mango purée
a thin mango slice, to garnish

serves 1

Add all the ingredients to a shaker filled with ice. Shake sharply and strain into a frosted margarita glass. Garnish with a thin slice of mango.

piñarita

The combination of pineapple and tequila results in a truly tropical flavour. I will allow you to decorate it lavishly, despite my open disdain for garish garnishes!

Add all the ingredients to a blender with two scoops of crushed ice and blend for 20 seconds. Pour into a hurricane glass, garnish with a thin slice of pineapple and serve.

50 ml/2 oz. gold tequila
4 teaspoons triple sec
4 teaspoons fresh lime juice
25 ml/1 oz. pineapple juice
a thin fresh pineapple slice, to garnish

serves 1

The fresh raspberries and Chambord in this drink team up to provide a fruity punch that almost masks the flavour of its base spirit. Don't be deceived, there's still plenty of tequila in here!

red cactus

50 ml/2 oz. Sauza Extra Gold tequila

4 teaspoons triple sec

4 teaspoons Chambord

35 ml/1½ oz. fresh lime juice

4 fresh raspberries, plus 2 to garnish

a lime wedge, to garnish

serves 1

Add all the ingredients to a blender with two scoops of crushed ice and blend for 20 seconds. Pour into a margarita, coupette or hurricane glass. Garnish with a wedge of lime and two raspberries.

raspberry torte

A successful cocktail needs to appeal at all levels. This one looks great on the eye, has a fresh lime and berry fragrance on the nose and, if you can ever bring yourself to consume your work of art, delights the taste buds.

50 ml/2 oz. gold tequila

4 teaspoons Cointreau

4 teaspoons fresh lime juice

50 ml/2 oz. raspberry purée

serves 1

Add the first three ingredients to a blender with two scoops of crushed ice and blend for 20 seconds. Pour half the mixture into a margarita or wine glass. Gently layer the raspberry purée over the surface of the drink to create a thin red line. Add the remaining margarita mix over the top and serve.

orange daiquiri

The Orange Daiquiri substitutes the sweet Martinique rum called Creole Shrub for the Cuban rum of the Original Daiquiri so uses a little less sugar syrup to keep that delicate balance of sharp and sweet.

50 ml/2 oz. Creole Shrub rum
4 teaspoons fresh lime juice
1 barspoon sugar syrup

serves 1

Add all the ingredients to a shaker filled with ice. Shake and strain into a frosted martini glass.

50 ml/2 oz. golden rum
12.5 ml/½ oz. fresh lime juice
2 barspoons sugar syrup

serves 1

original daiquiri

This classic cocktail was made famous at the El Floridita restaurant, Havana, early in the 20th century. Once you have found the perfect balance of light rum (traditionally Cuban), sharp citrus juice and sweet sugar syrup, stick to those measurements exactly.

Add all the ingredients to a shaker filled with ice. Shake and strain into a frosted martini glass.

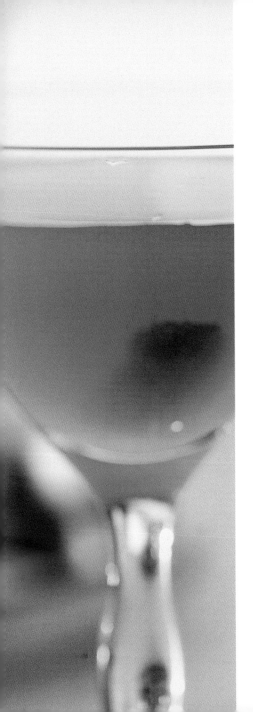

hemingway daiquiri

Legend has it that Hemingway was allergic to sugar so this drink was devised for him using maraschino liqueur as a sweetener (the sugar was returned to the drink when made for anyone other than the man himself!).

35 ml/1½ oz. white rum
1 teaspoon maraschino liqueur
2 teaspoons grapefruit juice
1 tablespoon sugar syrup
2 teaspoons fresh lime juice

Add all the ingredients to a shaker filled with ice. Shake sharply and strain into a frosted martini glass.

serves 1

mulato daiquiri

For those of you who like a more mellow daiquiri, experiment with aged rums until you find one that balances perfectly with the sugar, lime and your mood.

50 ml/2 oz. aged Cuban rum
(such as Bacardi 8 Year Old rum)
4 teaspoons fresh lime juice
2 barspoons sugar syrup
a dash of crème de cacao
(optional)

Add all the ingredients to a shaker filled with ice. Shake sharply and strain into a frosted martini glass.

serves 1

smashes, fixes & sours

Although mandarin season is traditionally winter, like lemons and limes, mandarins are now available most of the year. This is actually the perfect summertime barbecue cocktail – it seems to work well with smoky grilled food. Use tangerines or even oranges when mandarins are unavailable.

mandarin caprioska

1 mandarin, cut into wedges
fresh mint leaves, torn
2 tablespoons triple sec
2 tablespoons vodka
tonic water, to top up

serves 1

Drop the mandarin wedges and mint leaves into a chilled glass with ice, squeezing the mandarin wedges as you go. Pour over the triple sec and vodka, then top up with tonic water to serve.

Cachaça, a spirit indigenous to Brazil, is distilled directly from the juice of sugar cane. The Caipirinha has made cachaça popular in many countries.

caipirinha

1 lime, cut into wedges
2 brown sugar cubes
50 ml/2 oz. cachaça
sugar syrup, to taste

serves 1

Drop the lime wedges and sugar cubes into an old-fashioned glass, squeezing the limes as you go, then pound well with a pestle. Fill the glass with crushed ice and add the cachaça. Stir vigorously and add sugar syrup, to taste. Serve with two straws.

mojito

Guaranteed to whisk you away to warmer, tropical climes, the Mojito is one of Cuba's oldest cocktails. The origin of the name is thought to come from the African word 'mojo', which means to cast a little spell.

5 fresh mint sprigs, plus 1 to garnish
50 ml/2 oz. golden rum
a dash of fresh lime juice
2 dashes of sugar syrup
soda water/club soda, to top up

serves 1

Put the mint in a highball glass, add the rum, lime juice and sugar syrup and pound with a barspoon until the aroma of the mint is released. Add crushed ice and stir vigorously until the mixture and the mint is spread evenly. Top with soda and stir again. Garnish with more mint and serve.

mint julep

The Mint Julep originated in
the American Deep South.
Try substituting dark rum
or brandy for the bourbon.

5 fresh mint sprigs
2 sugar cubes
50 ml/2 oz. bourbon

serves 1

Crush the mint and sugar cubes
in the bottom of a glass. Fill the
glass with crushed ice and add the
bourbon. Stir the mixture vigorously
with a barspoon and serve.

cowboy hoof

The colour of this drink alone is worth the effort. Pay attention when straining the mixture as bits of mint sticking to the teeth are never attractive!

12 fresh mint leaves
2 teaspoons sugar syrup
65 ml/2¾ oz. gin
a fresh mint sprig, to garnish

serves 1

Add all the ingredients to a shaker filled with ice. Shake and strain through a sieve into a frosted martini glass. Garnish with a sprig of mint.

black bird

The Black Bird is not a spur-of-the-moment type of drink. The work put in beforehand is in equal proportion to the look of amazement on its drinker's face. The Cointreau and the brandy in the mix draw all the juices out of the berries and they combine with the alcohol in a most un-alcoholic way. This is a drink to be wary of.

berry mix (see right)
50 ml/2 oz. lemon vodka
25 ml/1 oz. fresh lemon juice
4 teaspoons Cointreau

serves 1

Place a scoop of berry mix into a frosted martini glass, press down. Add the remaining ingredients to a shaker filled with ice. Shake sharply then gently strain into the glass.

Berry mix: Add a punnet of each of the following: fresh strawberries, raspberries, blueberries and cranberries to a container. Add 25 ml/1 oz. brandy, 25 ml/1 oz. Cointreau and 500g/2½ cups caster/superfine sugar. Stir once and leave overnight. Stir once more before using.

A classic cocktail that can take whatever time throws at it. Choose red Bordeaux or Cabernet-Merlot blends for the claret.

claret cobbler

a lemon slice
a lime wedge
an orange wheel
2 tablespoons claret or port
25 ml/1 oz. vodka
25 ml/1 oz. crème de framboise

serves 1

Muddle the fruit in a shaker. Add the remaining ingredients, shake sharply and strain through a sieve into a rocks glass.

a fresh pineapple slice
an orange wheel
a lemon wheel
a dash of sugar syrup
champagne, to top up
a fresh mint sprig,
to garnish

serves 1

champagne cobbler

Champagne works with many complex flavours. If the fruit is not as ripe as it could be, add a dash more sugar syrup to encourage the flavour.

Muddle the fruit together in a rocks glass. Add crushed ice and the sugar syrup and gently top with champagne. Stir gently and garnish with a sprig of fresh mint.

port cobbler

Port has long been excluded from the world of contemporary cocktails simply because it is perceived as 'fuddy duddy'. However, its full flavour works well in many cocktails.

an orange wheel
a lemon wheel
a fresh pineapple slice,
plus 1 to garnish
75 ml/3 oz. ruby port
2 dashes of orange curaçao

serves 1

Muddle the fruit in a mixing glass, add the other ingredients and stir well. Strain into a rocks glass filled with crushed ice. Garnish with a slice of pineapple and serve.

A lesser-known cocktail that uses cachaça. This one is blended and, as a result of the greater dilution, not as potentially wobble inducing!

passion fruit batida

25 ml/1 oz. cachaça
25 ml/1 oz. passion fruit juice
25 ml/1 oz. fresh pineapple juice
a dash of passion fruit syrup
a dash of lime syrup
a dash of fresh lime juice
lime wedges, to garnish

serves 1

Add all the ingredients to a blender and blend. Strain into a highball glass over crushed ice. Garnish with wedges of lime.

This is a drink for the more adventurous! It is essential that a dark beer is used.

lagerita

1 lime, cut into 4
25 ml/1 oz. Centenario Añejo tequila
1 brown rock sugar cube
Negra Modello, or other dark beer, to top up

serves 1

Drop the lime quarters into a highball glass, squeezing as you go. Add the tequila and the sugar cube and muddle using a barspoon. Fill the glass with ice and add the dark beer. Muddle again, ensuring as much of the sugar as possible has dissolved. Serve.

The Fresca was invented to be served long with lemonade as a refreshing summer drink, but for every drinker who wants their thirst quenched there will always be two who want their socks knocked off! See below and opposite for a choice of ingredients.

fresca

basil & honey

50 ml/2 oz. vodka

a dash of fresh lime juice

a dash of grapefruit juice

2 fresh basil sprigs, crushed

1 teaspoon honey

a fresh basil leaf, to garnish

serves 1

Add all the ingredients to a shaker filled with ice. Shake sharply, then strain through a sieve into a frosted martini glass. Garnish and serve.

orange & pear

50 ml/2 oz. vodka
a dash of fresh lime juice
a dash of grapefruit juice
an orange slice, crushed
a pear slice, crushed
an orange zest, to garnish

serves 1

port & blackberry

50 ml/2 oz. vodka
12.5 ml/½ oz. port
a dash of fresh lime juice
a dash of grapefruit juice
4 fresh blackberries, plus 2 to garnish

serves 1

This is a perfect cocktail for drinking on a sunny deck in the cool of an early evening.

gin bramble

50 ml/2 oz. gin
25 ml/1 oz. fresh lime juice
2 teaspoons sugar syrup
25 ml/1 oz. crème de mure
a lemon slice and a fresh blackberry, to garnish

serves 1

Add the gin, lime juice and sugar syrup to a shaker filled with ice. Shake and strain into a rocks glass. Fill with crushed ice and pour in the crème de mure gently so that the liquid sinks to the bottom of the cocktail. Garnish with a slice of lemon and a blackberry.

This is a wonderful long cocktail – warm and comforting with its dark rum base but also zingy and refreshing with the tried and tested partnership of lime and ginger beer.

dark & stormy

50 ml/2 oz. dark rum
spicy ginger beer, to top up
4 lime wedges

serves 1

Build the rum and ginger beer into a rocks glass filled with ice. Drop the lime wedges into the glass, squeezing as you go. Stir gently and serve.

You may find variations of Lynchburg Lemonde using triple sec or Cointreau as the sweetening agent. This recipe uses caster/superfine sugar for its coarseness and fresh lemon wedges muddled together for a more 'rustic' variation.

lynchburg lemonade

2 lemon wedges
2 barspoons caster sugar
50 ml/2 oz. Jack Daniels
clear sparkling lemonade,
to top up

serves 1

Muddle the lemon and sugar together in a highball glass. Add ice and the remaining ingredients. Stir gently and serve.

One of the most famous of all rum-based drinks, this was reputed to have been invented by an army officer in Cuba shortly after Coca Cola was first produced in the 1890s.

cuba libre

50 ml/2 oz. white rum
½ lime, cut into 4
cola, to top up

serves 1

Pour the rum into a highball glass filled with ice. Drop the lime wedges into the glass, squeezing as you go. Top with cola and serve.

boston sour

The classic sour is made with Scotch, but the bourbon used in this recipe gives the drink a delicious vanillary sweetness.

50 ml/2 oz. bourbon
25 ml/1 oz. fresh lemon juice
2 barspoons sugar syrup
2 dashes of Angostura bitters
a dash of egg white
a lemon slice and a maraschino cherry, to garnish

serves 1

Add all the ingredients to a shaker filled with ice. Shake sharply and strain into a rocks glass filled with ice. Garnish with a slice of lemon and a maraschino cherry.

sour italian

A cocktail made completely
from Italian ingredients,
the Sour Italian makes
a good aperitif.

25 ml/1 oz. Campari
12.5 ml/½ oz. Strega
12.5 ml/½ oz. Galliano
25 ml/1 oz. fresh lemon juice
12.5 ml/½ oz. cranberry juice
12.5 ml/½ oz. sugar syrup
a dash of egg white
2 dashes of Angostura bitters

serves 1

Add all the ingredients to a shaker
filled with ice. Shake and strain into
a wine glass.

If you want to add that special touch to your cocktail and don't mind putting in a bit of work, then infusing blueberry into your amaretto is well worth the effort.

blueberry amaretto sour

50 ml/2 oz. blueberry-infused amaretto (see below)
25 ml/1 oz. fresh lemon juice
1 tablespoon sugar syrup
a lemon slice and 2 fresh blueberries, to garnish (optional)

serves 1

Blueberry-infused amaretto: Pierce ten blueberries with a knife and place them in a bottle of amaretto. Leave them for a few days and taste. You may want to strain the mixture before using it.

Add the infused amaretto and the remaining ingredients to a shaker filled with ice. Shake sharply and strain into a glass filled with ice. Garnish with a slice of lemon and two blueberries.

The words Midori and sour might not normally sit too happily together, but shake this one hard, go gentle on the sugar syrup and you'll have a great tasting, well-balanced and dramatic-looking cocktail.

midori sour

50 ml/2 oz. Midori
25 ml/1 oz. fresh lemon juice
1 tablespoon sugar syrup
a dash of egg white
a lemon wheel, to garnish

serves 1

Add all the ingredients to a shaker filled with ice. Shake sharply and strain into a wine glass filled with ice. Garnish with a lemon wheel and serve.

Pisco, like cachaça, brings to light some of the delights that are South American spirits. Tinker with the amounts of lemon and sugar you put in this cocktail to achieve your own perfect balance.

pisco sour

50 ml/2 oz. pisco
4 teaspoons fresh lemon juice
1 tablespoon sugar syrup
a dash of egg white
2 dashes of Angostura bitters
an orange zest, to garnish

serves 1

Add all the ingredients to a shaker filled with ice. Shake sharply and strain into a flute glass filled with ice. Squeeze a piece of orange zest over the surface and drop into the drink. Serve.

highballs, coolers
& punches

The creation of the Moscow Mule woke us up to the godsend that is ginger beer. It lends the Mule its legendary kick and an easy spiciness.

moscow mule

50 ml/2 oz. vodka
½ lime, cut into 4
ginger beer, to top up

serves 1

Pour the vodka into a highball glass filled with ice. Drop the lime wedges into the glass, squeezing as you go. Top with ginger beer and stir with a barspoon. Serve.

Perfect for an afternoon in the sun. Try substituting dark rum or bourbon for the vodka for a delicious alternative.

strawberry mule

2 thin fresh ginger slices
3 fresh strawberries, plus
1 to garnish
50 ml/2 oz. vodka
12.5 ml/½ oz. crème de fraise de bois
a dash of sugar syrup
ginger beer, to top up

serves 1

Muddle together the ginger and the strawberries in a shaker. Add the vodka, fraise de bois and sugar syrup and shake, then strain through a sieve into a highball glass filled with ice. Top with ginger beer, stir, garnish with a strawberry and serve with two straws.

Try this variation of the Moscow Mule (see page 140) – great for an after-dinner drink.

brazilian mule

25 ml/1 oz. vodka
12.5 ml/½ oz. peppermint schnapps
12.5 ml/½ oz. Stone's ginger wine
25 ml/1 oz. espresso coffee
a dash of sugar syrup
ginger beer, to top up
2 coffee beans, to garnish

serves 1

Add the vodka, peppermint schnapps and ginger wine to a shaker filled with ice. Pour in the espresso coffee and sugar syrup to taste. Shake and strain into a highball glass filled with ice and top with ginger beer. Garnish with two coffee beans and serve with two straws.

Don't get too carried away trying to get the spiral of lemon either too long or too similar to a horse's neck – after all it's how the drink tastes that's important!

horse's neck

50 ml/2 oz. bourbon
ginger ale, to top up
a lemon spiral, to garnish

serves 1

Build the ingredients into a highball glass filled with ice. Drape the lemon spiral into the glass and over the edge. Serve with two straws.

Although many 'real' cocktail drinkers disapprove of elaborate fruit salad-type garnishes, Pimm's has to be the one concession! Surprisingly, the tastiest addition to this drink is the cucumber, but try adding some sliced apple, too. This recipe doesn't include limes as the strong citrus juice too can be overwhelming.

pimm's cup

50 ml/2 oz. Pimm's No. 1
250 ml/1 cup clear
sparkling lemonade
75 ml/3 oz. ginger beer
a cucumber slice
a lemon slice
an orange slice
a fresh strawberry
a fresh mint sprig

serves 1

Build all the ingredients into a highball glass filled with ice. Stir gently and serve with two straws.

Why this cocktail is named Madras is a mystery, but it's especially refreshing when created with fresh orange juice. Perhaps it will become the mouth cooler of choice for curry-lovers!

madras

50 ml/2 oz. vodka
cranberry juice, to top up
fresh orange juice, to top up
an orange slice, to garnish

serves 1

Pour the vodka into a highball glass filled with ice. Top with equal amounts of cranberry juice and orange juice and garnish with a slice of orange. Serve with a straw.

A twist on the breeze format using flavoured vodka and fresh juices. There are a number of variations on this theme due to the ever-growing number of flavoured vodkas on the market these days.

tropical breeze

50 ml/2 oz. Wyborowa Melon vodka
cranberry juice, to top up
fresh grapefruit juice, to top up

serves 1

Pour the melon-flavoured vodka into a highball glass filled with ice. Top with equal amounts of cranberry and fresh grapefruit juice.

This is a great morning drink for summer. Simple to make and really refreshing but a few glasses will make you feel pleasantly sleepy, so watch you don't end up crawling back into bed.

sea breeze

150 ml/⅔ cup pure pink grapefruit juice
300 ml/1¼ cups pure cranberry juice
100 ml/4 oz. vodka
1 lime, cut into wedges

serves 2

Pour the fruit juices and vodka into a shaker filled with ice. Squeeze over a couple of lime wedges. Shake and strain into two highball glasses and add a lime wedge to each before serving.

50 ml/2 oz.
demerara rum

1 tablespoon orange
curaçao

1 tablespoon apricot
brandy

4 teaspoons fresh
lemon juice

4 teaspoons fresh
lime juice

a dash of Angostura
bitters

4 teaspoons orgeat
syrup

a fresh mint sprig,
to garnish

serves 1

jamaican breeze

The Jamaican Breeze is testament to Jamaican rum's ability to hold its own when mixed with a selection of flavours.

2 fresh ginger slices
50 ml/2 oz. white rum
75 ml/3 oz. cranberry juice
75 ml/3 oz. fresh pineapple juice

serves 1

Pound the fresh ginger and rum together in the bottom of a shaker with a barspoon or muddler, then add ice and the remaining ingredients. Shake and strain into a highball glass filled with ice.

mai tai

This cocktail has many variations. A thick, dark rum should be used along with all the fruit-based ingredients that lend it its legendary fruitiness.

Add all the ingredients to a shaker filled with ice. Shake and strain into an old-fashioned glass filled with ice. Garnish with a sprig of mint and serve with straws.

planter's punch

A Planter's Punch recipe can never be forgotten since Myers has very kindly put the recipe on the back label of its rum bottle. A great favourite for parties because it can be made in advance.

50 ml/2 oz. Myers rum
2 tablespoons fresh lemon juice
50 ml/2 oz. fresh orange juice
a dash of sugar syrup
soda water/club soda, to top up
an orange slice, to garnish

serves 1

Pour all the ingredients, except the soda, into a shaker filled with ice. Shake and strain into a highball glass filled with ice. Top up with soda and garnish with a slice of orange.

t-punch

Perfect for a hot summer day, the T-Punch is a refreshing drink, which can be made with more lime or more sugar, according to taste.

Place the sugar cube in the bottom of an old-fashioned glass. Drop the lime wedges into the glass, squeezing as you go. Pound with a pestle to break up the sugar. Add the rum and ice, then top up with soda. Stir and serve.

1 brown sugar cube
1 lime, cut into 8
50 ml/2 oz. white rum
soda water/club soda, to top up

serves 1

salty mexican dog

This tequila variation on the Salty Dog can cut through the fog of any hangover with its trinity of grapefruit, salt and vodka. Add a dash of hibiscus cordial (see page 57) for a sweetened variation.

50 ml/2 oz. tequila
200 ml/¾ cup grapefruit juice
a lime wedge, to garnish
salt, for the glass

serves 1

Add the tequila to a glass filled with ice and rimmed with salt. Top with the grapefruit juice and garnish with a lime wedge.

rum runner

The Rum Runner is a delicious example of rum's affinity with fresh juices as we've seen over the years in the classic Tiki cocktails and punches of Don the Beachcomber.

25 ml/1 oz. white rum
25 ml/1 oz. dark rum
freshly squeezed juice of ½ a lime
1 tablespoon sugar syrup
150 ml/⅔ cup fresh pineapple juice

serves 1

Add all the ingredients to a shaker filled with ice. Shake sharply and strain into a highball glass filled with crushed ice.

A cocktail synonymous with the 1970s, bad hair, lava lamps and cheesy cocktails. Try modernizing the recipe by using Chambord instead of the grenadine for more depth. Alternatively, swallow your pride, slip into your flares and enjoy.

tequila sunrise

50 ml/2 oz. gold tequila
200 ml/¾ cup fresh orange juice
4 teaspoons grenadine
an orange slice, to garnish

serves 1

Build the tequila and the orange juice into a highball glass filled with ice. Gently pour the grenadine down the inside of the glass so the syrup fills the bottom. Garnish with a slice of orange and serve with two straws.

The story goes that Harvey, a Californian surfer who had performed particularly badly in an important contest, visited his local bar to drown his sorrows. He ordered his usual screwdriver – only to decide that it wasn't strong enough for what he had in mind. Scanning the bar for something to boost his drink, his eyes fell on the distinctively shaped Galliano bottle, a shot of which was then added to his drink as a float.

harvey wallbanger

50 ml/2 oz. vodka
12.5 ml/½ oz. Galliano
fresh orange juice, to top up
an orange slice, to garnish

serves 1

Build all the ingredients into a highball glass filled with ice. Stir and serve with a slice of orange.

The botanicals in the gin get a bit of an unexpected boost from the elderflower, making this a delicate cocktail full of floral flavours.

elderflower collins

50 ml/2 oz. gin
4 teaspoons fresh lemon juice
1 tablespoon elderflower cordial
soda water/club soda, to top up
a lemon slice and a fresh mint sprig, to garnish

serves 1

Build all the ingredients into a highball glass filled with ice. Stir gently and garnish with a slice of lemon and a sprig of fresh mint.

The Americano is a refreshing blend of bitter and sweet, topped with soda to make the perfect thirst quencher for a hot summer's afternoon.

americano

25 ml/1 oz. Campari
25 ml/1 oz. sweet vermouth
soda water/club soda, to top up
an orange slice, to garnish

serves 1

Build all the ingredients into a highball glass filled with ice. Stir and serve with a slice of orange.

raspberry rickey

This fresh fruit cooler always appeals due to the nature of the ingredients – there just seems to be something about raspberries in cocktails that everyone enjoys!

4 fresh raspberries, plus 1 to garnish

50 ml/2 oz. vodka

4 teaspoons fresh lime juice

a dash of Chambord

soda water/club soda, to top up

serves 1

Muddle the raspberries in the bottom of a highball glass. Fill with ice and add the remaining ingredients and stir gently. Garnish with a fresh raspberry and serve.

Try the Vodka Collins for a sharp, zingy, thirst quencher on a hot day. Be warned, it's easy to forget there is alcohol in the drink!

vodka collins

50 ml/2 oz. Vox vodka
4 teaspoons fresh lemon juice
1 tablespoon sugar syrup
soda water/club soda, to top up
a lemon slice, to garnish

serves 1

Build all the ingredients into a highball glass filled with ice. Stir gently and garnish with a slice of lemon.

50 ml/2 oz. vodka
4 teaspoons fresh lime juice
1 tablespoon white peach purée
a dash of crème de pêche
soda water/club soda, to top up
thin peach slices, to garnish

serves 1

peach rickey

A Peach Rickey is a fantastic summer cooler and the perfect way to use up a surplus of juicy peaches. Ripe peaches will yield the best results if you're making your own purée.

Build all the ingredients into a highball glass filled with ice. Stir gently and garnish with a thin slice or two of peach.

This has a distinctly Caribbean flavour. You could use golden rum but I prefer the slightly more delicate taste of white rum.

passion fruit rum punch

300 ml/1¼ cups white rum

150 ml/⅔ cup passion fruit pulp (from about 6 large ripe passion fruit)

150 ml/⅔ cup fresh orange juice

600 ml/2⅓ cups clear sparkling lemonade

serves 6

Put the rum, passion fruit pulp and orange juice in a large jug/pitcher and chill for 1 hour. Half-fill six tall glasses with ice, add the rum and fruit juice mixture and top up with lemonade. Serve immediately.

This summer punch is the perfect drink for a balmy evening, especially if you are lucky enough to find yourself sitting by the sea.

classic sangria

2 oranges, sliced

2 lemons, sliced

1–2 tablespoons caster/superfine sugar, to taste

2 x 750-ml bottles red wine

165 ml/⅔ cup Grand Marnier or other orange-flavoured liqueur

1 red apple, sliced into thin wedges

clear sparkling lemonade, to top up

serves 12

Place half the orange and lemon slices in a large jug/pitcher and sprinkle over the sugar. Leave to macerate for 15 minutes then add the wine and Grand Marnier and chill for 1 hour.

When ready to serve, add the apple wedges and remaining slices of orange and lemon. Add a few scoops of ice and top up with lemonade to taste. Stir and pour into tall glasses to serve, spooning a little fruit into each, if liked.

The Tennessee Teaser is a variation on the more familiar Cuba Libre (see page 133) – great for those who enjoy a sharp citrus taste softened a little with sugar.

tennessee teaser

4 tablespoons Jack Daniels, or other bourbon
4 teaspoons fresh lemon juice
1 tablespoon sugar syrup
cola, to top up
a dash of Angostura bitters

serves 1

Half-fill a glass with ice. Add the Jack Daniels, lemon juice and sugar syrup and top up with cola. Add a dash of bitters and serve immediately.

gingerella punch

750 g/1½ lb. mixed melon flesh, such as watermelon, honeydew and galia, diced
750-ml bottle ginger wine, such as Stone's or Crabbie's
dry ginger ale, to top up
a handful of small fresh basil leaves, to garnish

serves 12

Put the melon and ginger wine in a large jug/pitcher and chill for 1 hour.

When ready to serve, transfer to a punch bowl and add a few scoops of ice. Pour in the ginger ale to taste and add the basil leaves. Ladle into tumblers or wine goblets to serve, spooning a little melon into each, if liked.

slammers
& shooters

A great drink to get the party started. Easy to make and even easier to drink, this is a low-maintenance shooter that does its job with minimum bother.

kamikaze

50 ml/2 oz. vodka
4 teaspoons Rose's lime cordial
1 tablespoon triple sec

serves 2

Add all the ingredients to a shaker filled with ice. Shake very hard, strain into two shot glasses and serve.

Slammers are a style of drink that's always great entertainment at a party. A small word of warning though, they are pretty potent and should be consumed in moderation.

alabama slammer

2 tablespoons Southern Comfort or bourbon
chilled champagne, to top up

serves 1

Pour the Southern Comfort and champagne into a sturdy shot glass.

Place your hand over the top and then firmly but carefully slam the bottom of the glass on the counter top. The drink will fizz up and should be drunk immediately and all at once!

pousse café

Pousse Café literally means 'push coffee' and this was how it was originally served – as an accompaniment to coffee, to be sipped layer by layer alternately with the coffee.

grenadine
dark crème de cacao
maraschino liqueur
curaçao
green crème de menthe
Parfait Amour
Cognac

serves 1

Layer a small measure of each of the ingredients, one on top of the other, in the order given in a pousse café or tall shot glass.

pousse café 2

Another real labour of love. The Pousse Café 2 requires a steady hand and a steely resolve – especially if your guest pays little shrift to your hard work and chooses to down the drink 'in one'!

grenadine
anisette
Parfait Amour
yellow Chartreuse
green Chartreuse
curaçao
Cognac

serves 1

Layer a small measure of each of the ingredients, one on top of the other, in the order given in a pousse café or tall shot glass.

The Tequila Slammer is the ultimate machismo drink and one that needs to be handled with care. This one is more likely to be imbibed for the sensation rather than the taste. A variation is to replace the gold tequila and champagne with silver tequila and lemonade.

tequila slammer

50 ml/2 oz. gold tequila
50 ml/2 oz. chilled champagne

serves 1

Pour both the tequila and the chilled champagne into an old-fashioned glass with a sturdy base. Hold a napkin over the glass to seal the liquid inside. Sharply slam the glass down on a stable surface and drink in one go as the drink is fizzing.

los tres amigos

The salt, tequila and lime method is as ubiquitous as the margarita when it comes to tequila. Recite the immortal words: 'lick, sip, suck' – and enjoy!

a lime wedge
50 ml/2 oz. gold tequila
a pinch of salt

serves 1

Hold the lime wedge between the thumb and index finger. Pour the tequila into a shot glass and place the glass in the fleshy part of your hand between the same thumb and finger. Place a pinch of salt on the top of your hand next to the shot glass. In this order: lick the salt, shoot the tequila, and suck on the lime.

submarine

Forget those age-old constraints of spirit and chaser standing alone. Opt instead for the energy-saving Submarine and allow the tequila to seep gently from under its upturned shot glass and mingle with the beer before it hits the palate.

50 ml/2 oz. gold tequila
a bottle Mexican beer (such as Sol)

serves 1

Pour the tequila into a shot glass. Place the shot glass in an inverted beer glass so that it touches the base of the beer glass. Turn the beer glass the right way up so that the shot glass is upside down but the tequila is still inside. Gently fill the beer glass with the beer and serve.

B52

The B52 has reached the lofty peak of being regarded a classic within the drinks world. This shot is best drunk after dinner as it has a tendency to take the palate by storm.

4 teaspoons Kahlúa
1 tablespoon Bailey's
1 tablespoon Grand Marnier

serves 1

Layer each ingredient on top of each other over a barspoon in a shot glass.

B50 who

The 'who' refers to the top layer of the shot. Explain the basic rules of the layered shot to your guests and let them choose their own grande finale to the drink.

4 teaspoons Kahlúa
1 tablespoon Bailey's
1 tablespoon any spirit over 37.5%

serves 1

Layer the first two ingredients in a shot glass, then allow your guest to choose a spirit to layer on the top.

sangrita

This drink is the perfect way to savour a fine tequila. Try varying the Sangrita mix, by adding different amounts of orange juice and spices.

50 ml/2 oz. añejo tequila
Sangrita mix:
    25 ml/1 oz. orange juice
    25 ml/1 oz. fresh lime juice
    a dash of grenadine
    a dash of Tabasco sauce
    a dash of Worcestershire sauce

serves 1

Pour the tequila into a shot glass. Add the remaining ingredients to a separate shot glass and stir gently. This drink should be tasted tequila first, followed by the Sangrita mix.

detox

In the Detox, the combination of peach schnapps, cranberry juice and vodka is one that has been toyed with before, but layering the well-chilled ingredients allows the luxury of tasting them one at a time.

25 ml/1 oz. ice-cold peach schnapps
25 ml/1 oz. cranberry juice
25 ml/1 oz. ice-cold vodka

serves 1

Pour the ice-cold peach schnapps into a frosted shot glass. Over the back of a barspoon, carefully layer an equal measure of cranberry juice so that it sits on top of the schnapps. Over the top of the cranberry juice layer a similar amount of ice-cold vodka. Serve.

There are various ways to present this shooter – you can coat a lemon slice in sugar and lay it over the surface of the glass to bite into after the shot, or you can take it one step further and soak the lemon in Cointreau before coating it, then set it alight!

lemon drop

50 ml/2 oz. lemon vodka
4 teaspoons Cointreau
4 teaspoons fresh lemon juice
a sugar-coated lemon slice, to garnish (optional)

serves 1

Add all the ingredients to a shaker filled with ice. Shake very hard and strain into a shot glass.

The Purple Haze is a classic Kamikaze (see page 164) with a twist – a drink that belies its strength and will kick-start any evening's fun.

purple haze

1 white sugar cube
½ lime, cut into 4
25 ml/1 oz. vodka
a dash of Grand Marnier
25 ml/1 oz. Chambord

serves 1

Put a sugar cube and the lime wedges into a shaker and crush them together with a muddler or barspoon. Add the vodka and Grand Marnier. Fill the shaker with ice, then shake and strain the mixture into a chilled shot glass. Float a single measure of Chambord onto the drink and serve.

digestifs
& creamy cocktails

With its dark velvety body and creamy top, the Vodka Espresso was designed both to wake up and to calm down its recipient simultaneously.

vodka espresso

25 ml/1 oz. espresso coffee
50 ml/2 oz. vodka
a dash of sugar syrup
3 coffee beans, to garnish

serves 1

Pour the espresso coffee into a shaker, add the vodka and sugar syrup to taste. Shake the mixture sharply and strain into an old-fashioned glass filled with ice. Garnish with three coffee beans.

silver streak

Kummel is one of the least used liqueurs in cocktails, more's the pity. It has a distinctive, almost aniseed-like taste that comes from the caraway seeds used in its production and, as an added bonus, it promotes good digestion. For the best results keep both the vodka and the kummel in a fridge or freezer and pour them gently into a sturdy old-fashioned glass for the perfect after-dinner nightcap.

25 ml/1 oz. chilled vodka
25 ml/1 oz. kummel

serves 1

Pour the chilled vodka into a rocks glass filled with ice. Add the kummel, stir gently and serve.

black russian

The Black and White Russians are classics that have been on the scene for many years. They make stylish after-dinner cocktails with their sweet coffee flavour, which is sharpened up by the vodka.

50 ml/2 oz. vodka
25 ml/1 oz. Kahlúa
a stemmed cherry, to garnish

serves 1

Add both the ingredients to a shaker filled with ice. Shake and strain into a rocks glass filled with ice. Garnish with a stemmed cherry.

white russian

The White Russian, with its
addition of the cream float,
is great served as a nightcap.

50 ml/2 oz. vodka
25 ml/1 oz. Kahlúa
25 ml/1 oz. single/light cream
a stemmed cherry, to garnish

serves 1

To make a White Russian, make a
Black Russian (see left) then layer the
cream into the glass over the back of
a barspoon. As before, garnish with
a stemmed cherry.

A spectacular drink to serve but one that is best practised in the safe confines of the kitchen before trying it in front of an audience. Another tip for those of you who are itching to light up your favourite pewter tankards – unless they have heat-resistant handles, burnt fingers may be the result of your first attempt at this cocktail!

blue blazer

1 sugar cube
50 ml/2 oz. boiling water
50 ml/2 oz. whisky
grated nutmeg, to garnish

serves 1

Warm two small metal tankards. In one, dissolve the sugar in the boiling water. Pour the whisky into the other. Set the whisky alight and, as it burns, pour the liquid into the first tumbler and back, from one to another, creating a continuous stream of fire. Once the flame has died down, pour the mixture into a warmed old-fashioned glass and garnish with a sprinkling of grated nutmeg.

This one's purely for the colder months, when you are curled up in front of an open fire, preferably with some sort of small four-legged creature curled up in your lap!

rusty nail

2 tablespoons whisky
2 tablespoons Drambuie
an orange zest, to garnish

serves 1

Add both the ingredients to a glass filled with ice and muddle with a barspoon. Garnish with an orange zest.

The trick to this great digestif is not to go crazy with the cream. Sweetening the coffee does help the cream sit well, but if you don't take sugar it should still work – you'll just need a steadier hand.

irish coffee

35 ml/1½ oz Irish whiskey
double espresso
2 teaspoons sugar syrup
250 ml/1 cup double/heavy cream
3 coffee beans, to garnish

serves 1

Mix the whiskey, coffee and sugar to taste in a heat-resistant glass, making sure the coffee is piping hot. Gently layer the cream over the surface of the coffee, using a flat-bottomed barspoon or a teaspoon. Garnish with three coffee beans.

With the added kick of the vodka, you're looking at an after-dinner drink that will both caress your taste buds and lure you onto slippery slopes!

mudslide

25 ml/1 oz. vodka

25 ml/1 oz. Bailey's

25 ml/1 oz. Kahlúa

4 teaspoons double/heavy cream (optional)

unsweetened cocoa powder, to garnish

serves 1

Add all the ingredients to a shaker filled with ice. Shake sharply and strain into a glass filled with ice. Alternatively, add all the ingredients to a blender with a scoop of crushed ice and blend for 10 seconds. Pour into a rocks glass. Garnish with a sprinkling of cocoa powder.

hot toddy

The Hot Toddy, with its warming blend of spices and sweet honey aroma, is the perfect comforter and will soothe any aches, snuffles and alcohol withdrawal symptoms that your illness may have inflicted upon you. It's also a great life-saver for cold afternoons spent outside watching sport. Next time you have need to pack a Thermos flask of coffee, think again – mix up a batch of Hot Toddies, and see how much more popular you are!

5 whole cloves

2 lemon slices

50 ml/2 oz. whisky

25 ml/1 oz. fresh lemon juice

2 barspoons honey or sugar syrup

75 ml/3 oz. hot water

1 cinnamon stick

serves 1

Press the cloves into the slices of lemon and add them to a heat-resistant glass along with the rest of the ingredients. Stir well and serve.

The Brandy Alexander is the perfect after-dinner cocktail, luscious and seductive and great for chocolate lovers. It's important, though, to get the proportions right so that the brandy stands out as the major investor.

brandy alexander

50 ml/2 oz. brandy
12.5 ml/½ oz. brown or white crème de cacao
12.5 ml/½ oz. double/heavy cream
grated nutmeg, to garnish

serves 1

Add all the ingredients to a shaker filled with ice. Shake and strain into a frosted martini glass. Garnish with a sprinkling of grated nutmeg.

stinger

A great palate cleanser and digestif which, like brandy, should be consumed after dinner. The amount of crème de menthe used depends on personal taste: too much and the result is akin to liquid toothpaste, another palate cleanser, but without the same effects unfortunately.

50 ml/2 oz. brandy
25 ml/1 oz. white crème de menthe

serves 1

Add both the ingredients to a shaker filled with ice. Shake and strain into a frosted martini glass.

Try serving this one long with milk for
a less intense flavour. Grate some fresh
nutmeg over the surface of the drink to
add a whole new depth of taste.

godchild

25 ml/1 oz. vodka
25 ml/1 oz. Amaretto
25 ml/1 oz. double/
heavy cream
grated nutmeg, to
garnish (optional)

Add all the ingredients to a shaker
filled with ice. Shake sharply and
strain into a rocks glass filled with ice.

serves 1

This drink is quite simply the best-ever
example of how a drink should never be
judged by anything less than the sum of
its parts. If this cocktail doesn't taste like
your favourite festive pudding, you're
doing something wrong!

blood & sand

25 ml/1 oz. Scotch whisky
25 ml/1 oz. sweet vermouth
25 ml/1 oz. cherry brandy
25 ml/1 oz. orange juice

Add all the ingredients to a shaker
filled with ice. Shake sharply then
strain into a frosted martini glass.

serves 1

The Orange Brûlée is a dessert drink that should be savoured. You'll notice the caramelization process is not recommended – would you trust a bartender with a blowtorch?

orange brûlée

25 ml/1 oz. Grand Marnier
12.5 ml/½ oz. Amaretto
a dash of white crème de cacao
whipping cream, to top
thin strips of orange zest,
to garnish

serves 1

Add all the ingredients, except the cream, to a shaker filled with ice. Shake sharply then strain into a martini glass. Whip the cream and dollop gently over the surface of the drink. Criss-cross with thin strips of orange zest.

When set the challenge to create something special with Drambuie Cream, I thought I would bend the rules a little. Mixing citrus fruits with cream liqueurs isn't generally recommended for cocktails, but somehow this concoction resists the temptation to curdle.

lemon meringue

50 ml/2 oz. Cytrynowka vodka
4 teaspoons fresh lemon juice
12.5 ml/½ oz. Drambuie Cream
a dash of sugar syrup

serves 1

Add all the ingredients to a shaker filled with ice. Shake sharply then strain into a frosted martini glass.

piña colada

A sweet, creamy drink which, for a time, epitomized the kind of cocktail that 'real' cocktail drinkers disapproved of (compare a Piña Colada with a Dry Martini!). Today, cocktails are for everyone so there's no shame in ordering a Piña Colada at the bar.

50 ml/2 oz. golden rum
25 ml/1 oz. coconut cream
12.5 ml/½ oz. cream
25 ml/1 oz. fresh pineapple juice
a fresh pineapple slice, to garnish

serves 1

Add all the ingredients to a blender with a scoop of crushed ice and blend. Pour into a hurricane or highball glass and garnish with a thick slice of pineapple.

honey colada

Try the Honey Colada variation for a sweet surprise lurking at the bottom of the glass – only for the very sweet-toothed! Alternatively, use the Mexican liqueur Kahlúa as the base, for a light coffee taste.

For a Honey Colada, add 2 barspoons of honey or sugar syrup to a freshly made Piña Colada.

Mix up a creamy Surf Rider and you'll be transported to a Caribbean beach with crystal clear, turquoise waves lapping at the shore.

surf rider

60 ml/2½ oz. Malibu (coconut-flavoured rum)
60 ml/2½ oz. fresh pineapple juice
60 ml/2½ oz. coconut milk
a small handful of fresh mint leaves
4 teaspoons dark rum

serves 2

Add the Malibu, pineapple juice, coconut milk and mint to a blender with crushed ice and blend until smooth. Spoon the mixture into two chilled cocktail glasses and float the dark rum over the top by pouring it in over the back of a spoon. Serve immediately.

This variation slips down the throat as easily as its name rolls off the tongue. Ensure this drink has the right consistency (light and fluffy) by adding crushed ice bit by bit to the blender.

tequila colada

50 ml/2 oz. gold tequila

4 teaspoons coconut cream

2 teaspoons double/heavy cream

150 ml/⅔ cup pineapple juice

a fresh pineapple slice, to garnish

serves 1

Add all the ingredients to a blender with two scoops of crushed ice and blend for 20 seconds. Pour into a hurricane glass and garnish with a slice of pineapple.

35 ml/1½ oz. gold tequila

1 tablespoon white crème de cacao

1 teaspoon grenadine

1 tablespoon double/heavy cream

2 fresh raspberries, to garnish

serves 1

silk stocking

This tequila drink was invented during the 1920s in the USA, at a time when cocktails were often given names revelling in innuendo and sensuality.

Add all the ingredients to a blender with two scoops of crushed ice and blend for 20 seconds. Pour the mixture into a hurricane glass, garnish with two raspberries and serve with two straws.

grasshopper

An obvious combination of peppermint and cream, the Grasshopper is the perfect drink to accompany your after-dinner coffee.

25 ml/1 oz. white crème de menthe
12.5 ml/½ oz. green crème de menthe
25 ml/1 oz. single/light cream

serves 1

Add all the ingredients to a shaker filled with ice. Shake and strain into a frosted martini glass and serve.

golden cadillac

If the thought of this combination is too much for you, try replacing the crème de cacao with Cointreau to make another popular cocktail called the Golden Dream.

25 ml/1 oz. white crème de cacao
25 ml/1 oz. single/light cream
50 ml/2 oz. fresh orange juice
a dash of Galliano

serves 1

Add all the ingredients to a shaker filled with ice. Shake and strain into a martini glass and serve.

The Bronx cocktail dates back to the days of Prohibition, when gang bosses reigned and booze played an important part in the economy of the underworld. Different areas of New York became known for the special cocktails they offered, such as these specialities of the Bronx.

silver bronx

50 ml/2 oz. gin
a dash of dry vermouth
a dash of sweet vermouth
50 ml/2 oz. fresh orange juice
1 egg white

serves 1

Add all the ingredients to a shaker filled with ice. Shake vigorously and strain into a chilled cocktail glass.

golden bronx

Like the Manhattan (see pages 92–3), the Bronx has three variations: the dry, the sweet and the perfect. The Silver and Golden Bronx are variations on the perfect with the addition of egg white or egg yolk.

50 ml/2 oz. gin
a dash of dry vermouth
a dash of sweet vermouth
50 ml/2 oz. fresh orange juice
1 egg yolk

serves 1

Add all the ingredients to a shaker filled with ice. Shake vigorously and strain into a chilled cocktail glass.

hangover cures

This might sound like a strange combination, but it works! The Gazpacho is a wonderful variation on the Bloody Mary (see page 208).

gazpacho

50 ml/2 oz. pepper vodka
black pepper, to taste
200 ml/¾ cup gazpacho soup
chopped fresh herbs, to garnish

Add all the ingredients to a shaker filled with ice. Shake really hard and strain into a martini glass. Garnish with a sprinkling of chopped herbs.

serves 1

Red Snapper was the name given to the Bloody Mary in the 1940s when the original title was deemed too risqué. This recipe takes the name but the format has been adapted.

red snapper

50 ml/2 oz. gin
75 ml/3 oz. tomato juice
4 dashes of Tabasco
a pinch of celery salt
2 dashes of lemon juice
a pinch of ground black pepper
4 dashes of Worcestershire sauce
ground black pepper, to garnish

Add all the ingredients to a shaker filled with ice. Shake sharply then strain into a frosted martini glass. Garnish with a sprinkling of freshly ground black pepper.

serves 1

a dash of olive oil
1 egg yolk
a dash of Tabasco sauce
2 dashes of Worcestershire sauce
2 dashes of vinegar or
lemon juice
salt and pepper

serves 1

This is one of those drinks that you have to try at least once in your life. It is best drunk quickly 'in one' – for obvious reasons.

prairie oyster

Rinse a martini glass with the olive oil and carefully add the egg yolk. Add the seasoning to taste and serve.

Apples, strawberries and bananas are all packed with nutrients and healing properties, which makes this great-tasting drink a perfect morning-after cleanser!

liver recovery

2 green apples
6 fresh strawberries
1 banana

serves 1

Peel, core, top and tail the assembled fruits, as necessary. Put each of them through a juicer, collecting the resulting juice. Add the juices to a blender with a scoop of crushed ice and blend. Pour into a small highball glass and serve.

The Corpse Reviver will either ease your suffering completely or send you back to sleep!

corpse reviver

25 ml/1 oz. calvados
25 ml/1 oz. vermouth rosso
25 ml/1 oz. brandy
an orange zest, to garnish

Add all the ingredients to a shaker filled with ice. Shake and strain into a frosted martini glass. Garnish with an orange zest and serve.

serves 1

The Stormy Weather is well qualified to treat your hangover with its good measure of Fernet Branca, a very bitter digestif that is often used on its own as a hangover cure.

stormy weather

25 ml/1 oz. Fernet Branca
25 ml/1 oz. dry vermouth
2 dashes of crème de menthe
a fresh mint sprig, to garnish

Add all the ingredients to a shaker filled with ice. Shake and strain into a small highball glass filled with ice and garnish with a sprig of mint.

serves 1

vodka stinger

This gives your mouth a minty freshness that will at least banish any lingering night-before tastes.

50 ml/2 oz. vodka

a large dash of white crème de menthe

serves 1

Add both the ingredients to a shaker filled with ice. Shake and strain into a martini glass.

bloody mary

Curing hangovers can be painless, and should be enjoyable, too. The objective of a hangover cure is to get you back on that 'horse' straight away before you spend too much time reflecting on your early morning pledge never to drink again! The measurements below depend on personal likes and dislikes.

50 ml/2 oz. vodka

200 ml/¾ cup tomato juice

2 grinds of black pepper

2 dashes of Worcestershire sauce

2 dashes of Tabasco sauce

2 dashes of lemon juice

1 barspoon horseradish sauce

a celery stick, to garnish

serves 1

Add all the ingredients to a shaker filled with ice. Shake and strain into a highball glass filled with ice. Garnish with a celery stick.

mocktails

It's so simple, I defy anyone not to admit that this drink, when served ice cold and in the right proportions, is the only thing that almost beats a Ribena made just right!

cranberry cooler

soda water/club soda
cranberry juice
a lime wedge

serves 1

Fill a tall highball glass with crushed ice. Pour in equal parts of soda and then cranberry juice. Drop the lime wedge into the glass, squeezing as you go. Serve with a straw.

Variation: Grapefruit Cooler. As above only with freshly squeezed grapefruit juice and garnished with slices of citrus fruits.

The name is taken from the
words of the English nursery
rhyme 'Oranges and lemons
said the bells of St Clement's'.

st clement's

bitter lemon
fresh orange juice
a lemon slice, to garnish

serves 1

Build both ingredients (the bitter
lemon first) in equal parts into
a highball glass filled with ice. Stir
gently, garnish with a slice of lemon
and serve.

This one works both as a meal and a drink!
To make it alcoholic, add a large measure
of Bailey's, which adds a kick and makes
the drink even more viscous.

virgin banana colada

1 ripe banana,
reserving 1 slice to
garnish

4 teaspoons coconut
cream

2 teaspoons
double/heavy cream

150 ml/⅔ cup
pineapple juice

Add all the ingredients to a blender with a scoop
of crushed ice and blend for 20 seconds. Pour into
a hurricane glass and garnish with a banana slice.
Serve with two straws.

serves 1

I couldn't resist a reference to Australia's
most famous beach for this summertime
drink. After all, there are few better ways
of watching the world go by than sipping
fruit shakes or cocktails as the heat of the
day fades and the sun worshippers head
home for the night.

1 large fresh mango,
peeled, pitted and
diced

1 banana, sliced

250 ml/1 cup
pineapple juice

50 ml/2 oz.
raspberry syrup

serves 2

bondi rip

Add the mango, banana and pineapple juice to
a blender with six ice cubes and blend until smooth.
To serve, drizzle a little raspberry syrup down the
sides of two tall glasses, pour in the blended fruit
and ice mixture and stir well. Serve immediately.

There's nothing in the manual that says cocktails with no alcohol in them should be low maintenance or one-dimensional. This one is a way of saying thank you to anyone who has taken on the noble role of designated driver for the night.

virgin mojito

6 fresh mint sprigs, plus 1 to garnish
1 barspoon caster/superfine sugar
2 lime wedges
soda water/club soda, to top up
a dash of sugar syrup

serves 1

Muddle the mint, sugar and lime in a highball glass filled with ice. Top with soda and muddle gently. Add sugar syrup to taste, garnish with a sprig of mint and serve.

Quite simply, there is nothing more satisfying than enjoying a classic, thirst-quenching Iced Tea on a warm day.

iced tea

4 tea bags
2.4 litres/5 pints hot water
1 lemon, sliced
sugar, to taste

serves 4

Add the tea bags to a jug/pitcher of hot, but not boiling, water. Stir, remove the tea bags and leave the tea to cool and stand before adding fresh lemon slices and chilling in the fridge. Once chilled, pour the tea into four highball glasses filled with ice. Add sugar to taste and serve.

virgin mary

300 ml/1¼ cups tomato juice
2 grinds of black pepper
2 dashes of Tabasco sauce
2 dashes of Worcestershire sauce
2 dashes of fresh lemon juice
1 barspoon horseradish sauce
a celery stick, to garnish
(optional)

serves 1

Although this variation of the Bloody Mary is without vodka, it certainly doesn't suffer in the taste department, including as it does a wonderful combination of flavours.

Add all the ingredients to a shaker filled with ice. Shake and strain into a highball glass filled with ice. Garnish with a celery stick.

shirley temple

25 ml/1 oz. grenadine

ginger ale or clear sparkling lemonade, to top up
a lemon slice, to garnish

serves 1

A thirst quencher for the very sweet-toothed and, most appropriately, named after the famous Hollywood child actress.

Pour the grenadine into a highball glass filled with ice and top with either ginger ale or lemonade. Garnish with a slice of lemon and serve.

pussy foot

Try using freshly squeezed pineapple juice instead of grapefruit for a slightly sweeter variation.

150 ml/⅔ cup fresh orange juice
150 ml/⅔ cup fresh grapefruit juice
a dash of grenadine
2 dashes of fresh lemon juice

serves 1

Add all the ingredients to a shaker filled with ice. Shake and strain into a highball glass filled with ice.

old-fashioned lemonade

There's nothing quite like old school lemonade. On a hot day, try using soda water/club soda instead of water for that extra zing.

25 ml/1 oz. fresh lemon juice
50 ml/2 oz. sugar syrup
150 ml/⅔ cup water
lemon slices, to garnish

serves 1

Add all the ingredients to a shaker filled with ice. Shake sharply and strain into a highball glass filled with ice. Garnish with slices of lemon and serve.

This non-alcoholic refresher is a play on the classic cranberry, grapefruit and vodka cocktail Sea Breeze (see page 146) but with the cranberry juice frozen into ice cubes. It's fun and funky at the same time.

sea freeze

300 ml/1¼ cups cranberry juice
400 ml/1⅔ cups fresh grapefruit juice
old-fashioned lemonade, to top up
lime wedges, to garnish

serves 2

Pour the cranberry juice into a 12-hole ice cube tray and freeze for at least 4 hours.

Divide the cubes between two tall glasses and add the fresh grapefruit juice. Top up with lemonade and garnish with wedges of lime.

This refreshing mocktail is an Australian classic. The addition of the bitters is not only a good foil for the sweet drink but adds a pretty pink tinge.

lemon, lime & bitters

a handful of fresh mint sprigs
2 limes, each cut into 8
1 litre/2¼ pints clear sparkling lemonade
50 ml/2 oz. lime cordial
a dash of Angostura bitters

serves 6

Half-fill six tall glasses with ice and add a sprig of mint and two or three lime wedges to each one.

Pour in the lemonade and lime cordial and add a few drops of bitters to serve.

This vibrant and deliciously tangy juice is reminiscent of the classic Tequila Sunrise (see page 152) but without the alcohol.

orange sunset

6 oranges
2 pomegranates

serves 2

Peel the oranges, chop the flesh and press through an electric juicer into a jug/pitcher. Halve the pomegranates and, using a lemon squeezer, squeeze out the juice into a separate jug/pitcher.

Pour the orange juice into two ice-filled glasses or tumblers, then pour in the pomegranate juice in a thin stream. Serve immediately.

This colourful, fruity punch will delight children and adults alike. Of course for those who just love a little extra pizzazz, you could always add a shot or two of vodka!

cranberry & fruit punch

250 g/2 cups mixed fresh berries, such as strawberries, raspberries and blueberries
1 orange, sliced
2 litres/4½ pints cranberry juice
1 small cucumber, peeled, seeded and sliced
sparkling water or clear sparkling lemonade, to top up

serves 12

Put the berries, orange slices and cranberry juice in a large jug/pitcher and chill for 1 hour.

When ready to serve, add the cucumber and some ice and top up with sparkling water. Pour into tall glasses or tumblers to serve.

glossary

ABSINTHE A very strong, green or yellow spirit made from wormwood (*Artemisia absinthium* in Latin, which gives absinthe its name) and flavoured with other botanicals including anise.

ABV Alcohol by volume. The percentage of alcohol by volume (ABV) indicates the strength of an alcoholic beverage and is shown on the bottle's label. Wine, for example, is about 11% ABV.

AMARETTO An amber-coloured liqueur of Italian origin, made from apricots and almonds.

ANISETTE An anise-flavoured liqueur of French origin.

ARCHER'S PEACH SCHNAPPS A colourless, very sweet, peach-flavoured liqueur.

BACARDI A well-known brand of rum, which originated in Cuba in the 19th century. The company now produces a range of different rums but the Bacardi name is synonymous with its original white rum.

BAILEY'S IRISH CREAM An Irish whiskey and cream liqueur with a lower alcohol content than most liqueurs.

BITTERS A potent herbal or fruit-flavoured alcoholic essence added to drinks in tiny amounts for its distinctive flavour. The original and most widely used bitters, Angostura, was first produced in the 1820s and is now produced in Trinidad. It has a rum base and is flavoured with herbs but details of the recipe are a closely guarded secret. Peychaud's bitters is an American brand invented in the 18th century by Antoine Peychaud. Orange bitters is flavoured with orange peel and other botanicals; peach bitters is another type available.

BLENDING A cocktail-making technique, which involves combining ingredients using an electric blender.

BOTANICALS Fruits, herb and spices (for example juniper berries, citrus peel, cardamom, angelica and coriander seeds) widely used as flavourings in the manufacture of various spirits.

BOURBON See 'Whisky'.

BRANDY An alcoholic spirit distilled from grape wine (ordinary brandy) or fermented mash of fruit (fruit brandy like apricot and cherry brandy). Fruit brandy is also known as eau de vie and tends to be unaged. True brandy is produced in every wine-growing region of the world, but the best comes from France, for example Cognac and Armagnac. V.S. ('very special') or three stars on the label indicates the brandy has been aged for a minimum of 2½ years; V.S.O.P ('very special old and pale') or Reserve denotes brandy that has been aged for a minimum of 4½ years; Napoleon or X.O. ('extra old') denotes brandy that has been aged for at least 6½ years old.

BUILDING A cocktail-making technique, which involves pouring the liquid ingredients into a glass, one at a time.

CACHAÇA A Brazilian spirit distilled directly from the juice of sugar cane (unlike rum, which is distilled from the molasses).

CALVADOS An aged French apple brandy from Normandy.

CAMPARI A vivid red, bitter-tasting Italian aperitif made from the peel of Seville oranges, herbs and quinine and first created in the 19th century.

CANNELLA LIQUEUR A cinnamon-flavoured Italian liqueur.

CHAMBORD A French liqueur made from small black raspberries.

CHAMPAGNE A sparkling wine from the Champagne region of France. Sparkling wines produced elsewhere by the same method are labelled 'Méthode Champenoise' and include Cava (Spanish), Spumante (Italian) and Sekt (German).

CHARTREUSE A potent herb-based liqueur created by French Carthusian monks according to an ancient secret recipe. There are two versions – green is stronger than the yellow.

COCONUT CREAM/MILK Ingredients derived from fresh coconut, used in cooking as well as for cocktails.

COGNAC A high-quality French brandy from the Cognac region in the south-west of France, first produced in the 19th century.

COINTREAU A colourless French liqueur made from oranges and similar to curaçao.

CORDIAL A fruit concentrate, or syrup, usually diluted with water before being drunk. Elderflower cordial is made from the flowers of the elderflower tree; Rose's, the best-known brand of lime cordial, is made from West Indian limes. See also 'Liqueur'.

CRÈME DE BANANES A brandy-based liqueur made from bananas.

CRÈME DE CACAO A chocolate-flavoured liqueur, available in white (colourless) and brown versions.

CRÈME DE CASSIS A sweet liqueur of French origin made from blackcurrants, often simply referred to as 'cassis'.

CRÈME DE FRAISE A liqueur of French origin made from strawberries. Crème de fraise de bois is made from wild strawberries.

CRÈME DE FRAMBOISE A liqueur of French origin made from raspberries.

CRÈME DE MENTHE A very sweet peppermint liqueur of French origin, which comes in green and white (colourless) versions.

CRÈME DE MURE A liqueur made from wild blackberries, often interchangeable with Chambord.

CRÈME DE PÊCHE A liqueur made from peaches.

CREOLE SHRUB A sweet orange-flavoured rum from the West Indies.

CURAÇAO An orange-flavoured liqueur of Caribbean origin, made from Seville oranges and available in colourless, blue, orange and green versions.

DRAMBUIE A Scotch whisky liqueur flavoured with heather and honey. Drambuie Cream is the cream version of the liqueur.

EAU DE VIE See 'Brandy'.

FRANGELICO An Italian hazelnut liqueur, apparently created by an Italian monk, Fra Angelico, who lived in Piedmont in northern Italy in the 17th century.

FROSTING A cocktail-garnishing technique,

which involves decorating the rim of a glass with salt, sugar, cocoa powder or grated nutmeg.

FRUIT JUICE A soft drink made from fruit concentrate, water and sugar, or juice that has been freshly extracted from fruit. Stick to the type of juice the recipe calls for – a carton of juice is no substitute for freshly squeezed fruit juice nor vice versa.

GALLIANO A pale yellow, herb-based Italian liqueur.

GIN A colourless grain spirit flavoured with botanicals, the main one being juniper berries. Distilled gin is the best-quality gin; be aware that some cheap brands have been 'cold infused' rather than distilled. London dry gin is the most popular type of gin today, although sweeter gins like Old Tom gin were more popular in the past.

GINGER ALE A sweet, non-alcoholic ginger-flavoured fizzy drink.

GINGER BEER A slightly alcoholic drink made from fermented root ginger.

GINGER LIQUEUR A ginger-flavoured liqueur. Dutch brand, The King's Ginger Liqueur, is a good one to try.

GINGER WINE A grape-based wine flavoured with ginger, plus some other spices and herbs.

GOLDSCHLAGER A strong, cinnamon-flavoured Swiss liqueur containing 24-carat gold flakes.

GRAND MARNIER A Cognac-based, orange-flavoured French liqueur.

GRENADINE A sweet, red non-alcoholic syrup, originally made from pomegranates but now often artificially flavoured.

JACK DANIEL'S See 'Whisky'.

KAHLÚA A dark brown, coffee-flavoured Mexican liqueur.

KUMMEL A colourless Danish liqueur flavoured with caraway seeds and cumin.

LAYERING A cocktail-making technique, which involves very carefully pouring liqueurs of different densities on top of each other in a small narrow glass to make an attractive, multi-layered beverage like the B52 or a Pousse Café.

LIQUEUR Known as cordials in the USA, liqueurs are high-quality sweet spirits flavoured with the fruits, seeds, leaves or flowers of plants and often prettily coloured.

MANZANA VERDE A green liqueur with the refreshing taste of raw green apples.

MARASCHINO A non-alcoholic syrup flavoured with cherries.

MARASCHINO LIQUEUR A sweet colourless liqueur made from maraska cherries.

MEZCAL Unlike tequila, the production of which is strictly regulated, mezcal is distilled only once and can be made from any agave plant and in any region of Mexico. A bottle of mezcal often has a worm in the bottom.

MIDORI A bright green Japanese liqueur made from musk melons.

MUDDLING A cocktail-making technique, which involves using a barspoon or muddler to mash ingredients such as fruit and herbs in the bottom of a glass so as to release their flavour.

ON THE ROCKS Description of a drink that is served over ice, as opposed to 'straight up', which means served without ice.

ORANGE FLOWER WATER A flavouring made from orange blossom, used in cooking as well as in cocktails.

ORGEAT A milky non-alcoholic syrup flavoured with almonds.

OVERPROOF A description for very strong spirits with an ABV above the average of 40%.

PARFAIT AMOUR A purple-coloured, scented liqueur, made from brandy, oranges, lemons and herbs.

PERNOD A French anise-flavoured spirit, which turns a cloudy pale yellow when mixed with water.

PIMM'S NO. 1 The first of six different spirit-based Pimm's (only two of which are available today), this one is made from gin blended with herb extracts and quinine and was invented in London in 1840 by James Pimm.

PISCO A colourless South American spirit, distilled from the muscat grape and produced in Peru and Chile.

POIRE WILLIAM A pear-flavoured fruit brandy (see 'Brandy'). Liqueur de Poire William is less fiery than the Poire William eau de vie.

PORT A fortified wine made in the same way as sherry and available in several styles, for example tawny, ruby, vintage and white. Originally made only in Portugal, port is now produced in countries such as Australia, America and South Africa.

POUSSE CAFÉ A dramatic-looking cocktail in which various liqueurs of different densities are layered in a small narrow glass.

ROSE WATER A flavouring made from rose petals, used in cooking as well as in cocktails.

RUM A spirit distilled from molasses or directly from the fermented juices of sugar cane. There are hundreds of different rums, ranging in hue from light/white (colourless) through golden colours to dark brown. The majority of rums are produced in the Caribbean.

RYE See 'Whisky'.

SAKE A Japanese alcoholic drink, commonly referred to as 'rice wine'.

SAMBUCA A dry, anise-based Italian liqueur flavoured with elderberries. Black sambuca is a thicker and stronger tasting version.

SCHNAPPS A strong distilled colourless spirit, available plain or flavoured, for example apple, butterscotch, cherry, peach, pepper-mint and strawberry.

SHAKING A cocktail-making technique for thick ingredients that need thorough mixing, which involves combining ingredients together in a cocktail shaker.

SHERRY A fortified wine, available as dry (fino), medium and sweet (oloroso). Sherry was originally made only in the Jérez region of Spain, but is now produced in other regions of Spain and elsewhere in the world, for example the USA and South Africa.

SHOOTER A drink that is served in a shot glass and downed in one.

SLOE GIN A deep red/purple liqueur made from gin flavoured with sugar and sloes.

SOUTHERN COMFORT An American liqueur combining bourbon whiskey with peaches, oranges and herbs, created in New Orleans in the 1880s.

STIRRING A cocktail-making technique for clear drinks, which involves simply mixing the ingredients together in a mixing glass using a barspoon.

STREGA A yellow Italian liqueur with a citrus base and flavoured with herbs.

SUGAR SYRUP Also known as gomme syrup and sirop de gomme, this non-alcoholic syrup made from sugar is widely used in cocktail-making. Available commercially or can be made at home.

TEQUILA A Mexican spirit, distilled from the juice of the blue agave plant, one of 400 species of agave, and produced only in certain regions of Mexico. There are four varieties: silver, gold, rested and aged.

TIA MARIA A rum-based, coffee-flavoured Jamaican liqueur.

TRIPLE SEC A colourless orange-flavoured liqueur similar to Cointreau.

VERMOUTH A fortified wine made in both Italy and France, flavoured with herbs, sugar and caramel and available in sweet, dry, red and white versions. Kina Lillet, now known simply as Lillet, and Noilly Prat are highly regarded French vermouths. Cinzano and Martini & Rossi are well-known Italian brands.

VODKA Traditionally perceived as a colourless, tasteless and odourless grain spirit in the West, vodka is also available flavoured. Popular flavourings include bison grass (Zubrowka), blackcurrant, honey, lemon, lime, mandarin, melon, orange peel, pepper and raspberry. Vodka produced in the East yields more flavoursome results.

WHISKY (Scotch/Canadian) or whiskey (US/Irish) is a spirit distilled from grain, malt, sugar and yeast, first made in Scotland and Ireland more than 500 years ago. The various Scotch, Irish, Canadian and American whiskies are very different. Scotch whisky is either a single malt or a blend of malt and grain whiskies – mixtures of the same whisky from different years or of different types of whiskies. Irish whiskey is made with a mixture of malted and unmalted barleys and is less pungent than Scotch because the barley is dried in a different type of kiln. All Canadian whisky is blended rye whisky, of a uniform high quality and rather light in both colour and taste. Originally only from Bourbon County, Kentucky, USA, bourbon whiskey is made from at least 51 per cent corn and a blend of barley and rye or wheat, while American rye whiskey is made with at least 51 per cent rye. Jack Daniel's is a 'sour mash' whiskey produced at the Jack Daniel's distillery in Lynchburg, Tennessee, USA.

index

recipe credits

BEN REED

Americano
Anejo manhattan
Apple manhattan
Applejack
  martini
Apricot royale
Azure martini
B50 who
B52
Basil & honey
Bellini
Berry margarita
Bitter
  cosmopolitan
Black bird
Black bison
Black dog
Black Russian
Black velvet
Blood & sand
Blood martini
Bloody Mary
Blue blazer
Blueberry
  amaretto sour
Boston sour
Brandy
  Alexander
Brazilian mule
Breakfast martini
Caipirinha
Cajun martini
Champagne
  cobbler
Champagne
  cocktail
Champagne
  julep
Cherry martini
Churchill martini
Citrus martini
Claret cobbler

Classic
  cosmopolitan
Classic margarita
Classic martini
Conmemorativo
Corpse reviver
Cosmo royale
Cowboy hoof
Cranberry cooler
Cuba libre
Dark & stormy
Detox
Dry manhattan
Elderflower
  collins
French 75
French martini
Fresca
Gazpacho
Gibson
Gin bramble
Gin gimlet
Ginger
  champagne
Ginger
  cosmopolitan
Godchild
Golden Bronx
Golden cadillac
Gotham
Grasshopper
Green iguana
Harvey
  wallbanger
Hazelnut martini
Hemingway
  daiquiri
Herba Buena
Hibiscus
Honey colada
Horse's
Horse's neck
Hot toddy

Iced tea
Irish coffee
Jamaican breeze
James bond
Joe Average
Kamikaze
Kir royale
La margarita de
  le patron
Lagerita
Legend
Lemon drop
Lemon meringue
Liver recovery
Los tres amigos
Lynchburg
  lemonade
Madras
Mai tai
Mangorita
Martinez
Metropolis
Metropolitan
Mezcal margarita
Midori sour
Mint julep
Mojito
Montgomery
Moscow mule
Mudslide
Mulato daiquiri
Negroni
New Orleans fizz
New Orleans
  sazarac
Old-fashioned
Old-fashioned
  lemonade
Orange & pear
Orange brulée
Orange daiquiri
Original daiquiri
Passion fruit
  batida
Peach rickey
Pear martini
Perfect

manhattan
Pimms cup
Pina colada
Pinarita
Pink gin
Pisco sour
Planter's punch
Polish martini
Pomegranate
  martini
Pontberry
  martini
Port &
  blackberry
Port cobbler
Pousse café
Pousse café 2
Prairie oyster
Premium
  manhattan
Prickly pear
  margarita
Purple haze
Pussy foot
Raspberry
  martini
Raspberry rickey
Raspberry torte
Red cactus
Red snapper
Red star
Rossini
Royal gin fizz
Rude
  cosmopolitan
Rum runner
Rusty nail
Sake martini
Salty Mexican
  dog
Sangrita
Sapphire martini
Shirley temple
Sidecar
Silk stocking
Silver Bronx
Silver streak

Sloe gin fizz
Smoky martini
Sour Italian
St. Clements
Stinger
Stormy weather
Strawberry
  cosmopolitan
Strawberry mule
Submarine
Sweet
  manhattan
Tequila colada
Tequila rickey
Tequila slammer
Tequila sunrise
Tequilini
Thunderer
T-punch
Tres compadres
Triple gold
  margarita
Tropical breeze
Turkish chocolate
Ultimate martini
Vesper
Virgin banana
  colada
Virgin Mary
Virgin mojito
Vodka Collins
Vodka espresso
Vodka stinger
Vodkatini
White Russian

LOUISE PICKFORD

Alabama
  slammer
Bondi rip
Chocotini
Classic sangria
Cosmopolitan
  iced tea
Cranberry & fruit
  punch
Gingerella punch
Hollywood
  hustle
Iced pear sparkle
Lemon, lime &
  bitters
Mandarin
  caprioska
Orange sunset
Passion fruit rum
  punch
Sea freeze
Surf rider
Tennessee teaser

TONIA GEORGE

Blood orange &
  campari
mimosa
Sea breeze

photography credits

All photography William Lingwood
except page 224 by Ian Wallace